In School Together

In School Together

School-based Child Care Serving Student Mothers

A HANDBOOK

MICHELE CAHILL

J. LYNNE WHITE

DAVID LOWE

LAUREN E. JACOBS

Foreword by

MARIAN WRIGHT EDELMAN

ACADEMY FOR EDUCATIONAL DEVELOPMENT

SCHOOL SERVICES DIVISION

This handbook is based on a study funded by
the Women's Educational Equity Act Program,
United States Department of Education

Copyright © 1987 Academy for Educational Development

Library of Congress Cataloging-in-Publication Data

In school together.
Bibliography: p. 120.
1. School-based child care—United States.
2. Adolescent mothers—United States.
3. Child care—Study and teaching—United States.
4. Parenting—Study and teaching—United States.
I. Cahill, Michele, 1948-
LB3436.I5   1987   362.7'12   87-14338
ISBN 0-89492-061-8

Designed by Christopher Holme
Drawings by Giora Carmi
Produced by the Publishing Center for Cultural Resources, New York City
Manufactured in the United States of America

Contents

Foreword 7

Preface 9

Acknowledgments 11

School-based Child Care Centers Visited 12

CHAPTER ONE
Introduction 13

CHAPTER TWO
Need 17

CHAPTER THREE
Support Strategies 27

CHAPTER FOUR
Design 40

CHAPTER FIVE
Staff 48

CHAPTER SIX
Infant/Toddler Program 59

CHAPTER SEVEN
Programming for Mothers 71

CHAPTER EIGHT
The Center as a Learning Lab 82

CHAPTER NINE
Site and Space 84

CHAPTER TEN

Policies   93

CHAPTER ELEVEN

Funding   102

CHAPTER TWELVE

Management and Evaluation   113

CHAPTER THIRTEEN

Additional Resources for Program Planning   120

Charts

Sources of information on adolescent pregnancy and parenting   22

Community resources for support   29

Identifying key sources of support   36

Some developmental characteristics and appropriate playthings to make   62

Sample daily report form   77

State child care center licensing offices   86

Sample outline of initial funding proposal   108

Foreword

Each year almost 500,000 American teenagers give birth to children. While our first priority must be reducing teen pregnancy rates, we must also provide the support that those girls who have already had babies need to become independent adults. Self-sufficiency for any young person depends to a large degree on the completion of her education. However, staying in school—a regular school or an alternative high school—or participating in a vocational training course is extraordinarily difficult for a parenting teenager, one who has all the usual problems of a girl that age *plus* the special challenges of being a mother and having responsibility for a small child. In order to successfully pursue further education, student mothers must have help with arranging for child care.

Obtaining child care is no easy task for a young mother who is also likely to be without the financial resources to purchase the services she needs. Teen parents with infants do not have a ready supply of child care options available to them. Most high schools still do not offer child care programs, and as a result, teens must seek infant care in their communities. They find a very bleak picture. Infant care is extremely hard to locate. It is in short supply because it is costly, requiring more staff than do child care programs serving older pre-school children. Whatever slots are available are eagerly sought by the growing number of mothers of all ages who have children under one and who are in the labor force. Moreover, teen parents with low or no incomes must receive help in meeting the costs of child care.

Study after study has identified child care as one of the most significant unmet needs of young parents. In 1982 *Public Health Reports* related that as far back as 1978, a nationwide study of teenage mothers and their babies in 125 large cities had found that the primary problem for young mothers was insufficient infant child care. A 1979 survey of 100 teen parents in the Boston area by the American Institute for Research also found child care assistance to be a critical service for teen mothers, and it determined that affordable child care for children under three was extremely hard to locate. A 1980 interview study by the Family Impact Seminar and the Alliance for Young Families in Massachusetts found that 50 percent of the young parents in the sample lacked consistent child care within their family networks. The majority of respondents viewed child care as essential to their participation in school, vocational training, or work and indicated that they would accept child care outside their families if it were available, particularly if provided in high schools.

An investment in child care assistance is crucial if young parents are to complete their education. If teen mothers do not have access to child care that they can trust and afford, they are unlikely to leave their children each day to return to high school to get their diplomas, to attend GED classes, or to enroll in vocational training. Instead, they will drop out to care for their children. Staying in school and completing their education is clearly connected to teens' abilities to become independent and productive adults, as well as to preventing repeat pregnancies.

Beyond the assistance that child care provides a mother in her effort to complete her education, a high-quality child care program for children of teen parents has a number of additional benefits. It can serve as a focus for organizing comprehensive support services for teen parents and their families. Such child care programs can help mothers delay second pregnancies, can enhance parenting skills, can address interfamilial stress, and can assure health, nutrition, or other supportive services.

The combination of help that can be organized in a school with a child care facility is especially powerful. The sort of one-stop service this school provides is particularly effective with young mothers who are easily overwhelmed by the competing demands made on them by baby, family, partner, teachers, and friends.

The advantages of child care at a school site cannot be overemphasized:

- Teen parents who are at home alone with their children and who are not studying or working are more likely to fill their lives with an additional child. The provision of supportive child care programs is likely not only to reduce school dropout but also to lower repeat pregnancy rates. The New Futures School in Albuquerque, New Mexico has operated a child care program for teen mothers since 1974. A 1981 follow-up study of students who participated during the past six years showed that almost all participants (82 percent) graduated from high school or obtained a General Equivalency Dipolma and that 31 percent of all these graduates obtained some post-secondary educational training. The director felt that child care was a key factor in keeping the repeat pregnancy rate to one-third the national average.
- Without alternative child care options, teen mothers often turn to their own mothers or other family members to provide child care while they continue their education. In some cases a grandmother or other relative, under such circumstances, feels she has to leave a full- or part-time job in order to care for the new infant. The loss of her income may jeopardize the well-being of the entire family.
- Child care centers organized to serve teenage mothers can offer parenting education that is particularly tailored to the needs and problems of young mothers. Without the opportunity to learn and apply new knowledge about infant stimulation, child development, and the critical role of parents, a student mother's child's emotional or physical growth may be retarded. Some children never recover or make up the ground lost during infancy.
- Good child care can also help to relieve some of the stress associated with teen parenting and reduce the potential for child abuse.
- Programs that include pregnant teens can help ensure healthy birth outcomes and healthy childhoods. School-based child care programs can start helping teens during pregnancy. Pregnant teens can attend parenting classes and receive nutrition education. Child care programs can also help them arrange for prenatal care. Pregnant teens who do not have good health and nutrition information are substantially more likely to have low-birthweight babies. In 1984, 14 percent of infants born to mothers under age 15 and 10 percent to mothers age 15–17 were born at low birthweight, as compared to 7 percent to older mothers. A teenage mother's child is more likely to be admitted to a hospital suffering from gastrointestinal infection in the early years. By linking teen parents to health services after birth, child care programs can reduce the health risks in a child's early years. Good child care can also provide families with nutrition education and at least one balanced meal a day.

Child care is a critical service which must be provided if we are to help move young parents toward independence and help their vulnerable children overcome the barriers that face them. Progress toward addressing the pressing needs of these young families has been far too slow. The programs presented in this well-researched volume represent some of the best efforts to move forward. But they alone can meet only a tiny percentage of the need. The models can and must be widely replicated. School administrators across this nation should carefully examine and use this invaluable resource to fulfill their mandate to provide *all* of our young people with the foundations upon which to build productive lives.

Marian Wright Edelman
President, Children's Defense Fund

Preface

IN SCHOOL TOGETHER is the first publication developed by the Academy for Educational Development's new Support Center for Educational Equity for Young Mothers. To serve as a resource to the thousands of policymakers, practitioners, and service providers working to improve educational opportunities and economic chances for women who bore their first child as a teenager, the Support Center will conduct research, produce reports, provide training, and offer technical assistance. Elizabeth McGee, an expert in the area of teenage pregnancy, is the director of the Support Center.

Staff at the center are prepared to work with educators on developing new approaches to assisting student mothers. Equity for these mothers can be guaranteed only when schools pursue affirmative action for their education. To succeed at school, student mothers must have access either to regular school courses and activities or to quality alternatives, personal assistance with support needs, and guidance on ways to pursue realistic plans for economic independence.

Beyond the equity issues at stake, it simply makes good sense for schools to adopt new approaches toward student mothers. Helping pregnant and parenting teenagers remain enrolled in school is an effective strategy for reducing dropout rates. Helping young parents maintain their commitment to educational advancement and appropriate childrearing practices is a service both to students and to their children, who soon will become students.

Schools' interventions on behalf of teenage mothers will have an impact on two generations of students. Thus the Support Center's work will focus on positive reforms for both young mothers and their children.

The Support Center is located in the School Services Division of the Academy for Educational Development. This division assists elementary and secondary school educators in maintaining effective schools for all students. Much of its work focuses on increasing the educational opportunities for minorities, girls, and low-income youth. To extend its efforts on behalf of female students, the division has taken on several new projects. The Urban Middle Schools Adolescent Pregnancy Prevention Program, under the direction of Michele Cahill, is the first of these projects, and the Support Center is the second.

The changing American family, with its increased financial demands on women, forces all institutions, but especially schools, to examine their roles and responsibilities. Failure to counter outmoded, unrealistic expectations regarding girls' interests and future roles contributes to many of the social problems that currently concern Americans—problems such as welfare dependency, teenage pregnancy, and poverty among children living in a female headed household. No greater challenge faces schools today than to redress the discrimination female students experience through policies and practices that reflect stereotyped and outdated ideas about women and girls.

Student mothers are particularly handicapped by these stereotypes, since they are reflected in school routines and curricula. For example, young mothers, with significant family responsibilities, do not fit the typical student profile and frequently cannot conform to many traditional school requirements. Furthermore, without the skills to pursue an occupation suitable for maintaining a household, most young mothers experience considerable economic instability throughout their lives.

School-based child care centers are one practical way for schools to help young mothers remain in school or return to school, complete their education, and acquire appropriate credentials for employment. This handbook provides information and practical suggestions on organizing and operating such a center.

We look forward to hearing from you to learn how we can more effectively help you assist young mothers in schools.

> Sharon L. Franz
> Vice President and Director
> School Services Division

Acknowledgments

Many school administrators, educators, and child care workers shared their knowledge, opinions, and daily experiences with us during the preparation of *In School Together: School-based Child Care Serving Student Mothers—A Handbook*. Without their participation we would have no tale to tell. They are among the pioneers—educational leaders who have identified the needs of teen mothers and creatively addressed their problems. We appreciate their generosity and wisdom and hope this guide will make it easier for them to help other people start and sustain school-based child care programs for young mothers.

The idea for the handbook and design of the project originated with Sharon L. Franz, director of the School Services Division at the Academy for Educational Development (AED). The guide is based on a site visit survey of six centers around the country coordinated by Sarah White and conducted by J. Lynne White, Grace Ibanez Friedman, and Urmila Acharya.

J. Lynne White, David Lowe, and Lauren E. Jacobs transformed the data on discrete centers into a coherent and proscriptive manuscript. Along with myself they are the principal writers of the guide. Elizabeth A. McGee, director of AED's Support Center for Educational Equity for Young Mothers, contributed many ideas about effective programming for young mothers and broadened our understanding of the problems they face. Judith R. Smith provided technical expertise on infant curriculum. Margaret Terry Orr, Kenneth Tewel, Donna Kiersbilck, Susan Oehrig, and Lyn Overholt reviewed drafts of the guide and provided helpful criticism on form and content from their perspectives as school principals, researchers, educational advocates, and social service and child care professionals. We appreciate their suggestions, many of which improved the clarity and focus of the guide. Our goal in developing this handbook has been to assist educators and advocates in meeting the needs of teen mothers and their children by providing a compilation of knowledge from the field. The many colleagues mentioned above strengthened this effort.

                                              Michele Cahill
                                              Associate Director for Adolescent,
                                                  Family, and Community Programs
                                              School Services Division
                                              Academy for Educational Development

School-based Child Care Centers Visited

The Academy for Educational Development conducted indepth studies of the following child care centers to gather the information on organization, program design, and implementation of quality child care in a school-based setting that served as the basis of this publication.

Center for Infant Development
  Elizabeth Board of Education
  Elizabeth High School
  630 South Street
  Elizabeth, NJ 07202

Crib Infant Care Center
  St. Louis Public Schools
  Vashon High School
  3405 Bell Avenue
  St. Louis, MO 63106

Murray-Wright Infant–Toddler Child Development Center
  Detroit Public Schools
  Murray-Wright Senior High School
  2001 West Warren Avenue
  Detroit, MI 48208

Polytechnic Child Care Center
  Fort Worth Independent School District
  Polytechnic High School
  1300 Conner Avenue
  Fort Worth, TX 76105

Rule High School Preschool/Parenting Learning Center
  Knoxville City Schools
  Rule High School
  1919 Vermont Avenue
  Knoxville, TN 37921

Living for the Young Family through Education (LYFE) Program*
  New York City Board of Education
  Bay Ridge High School
  350 67th Street
  Brooklyn, NY 11220

*Since the completion of research contained in this publication, this program and high school have been renamed Toddler Tech and High School for Telecommunication Arts and Technology, respectively.

CHAPTER ONE
Introduction

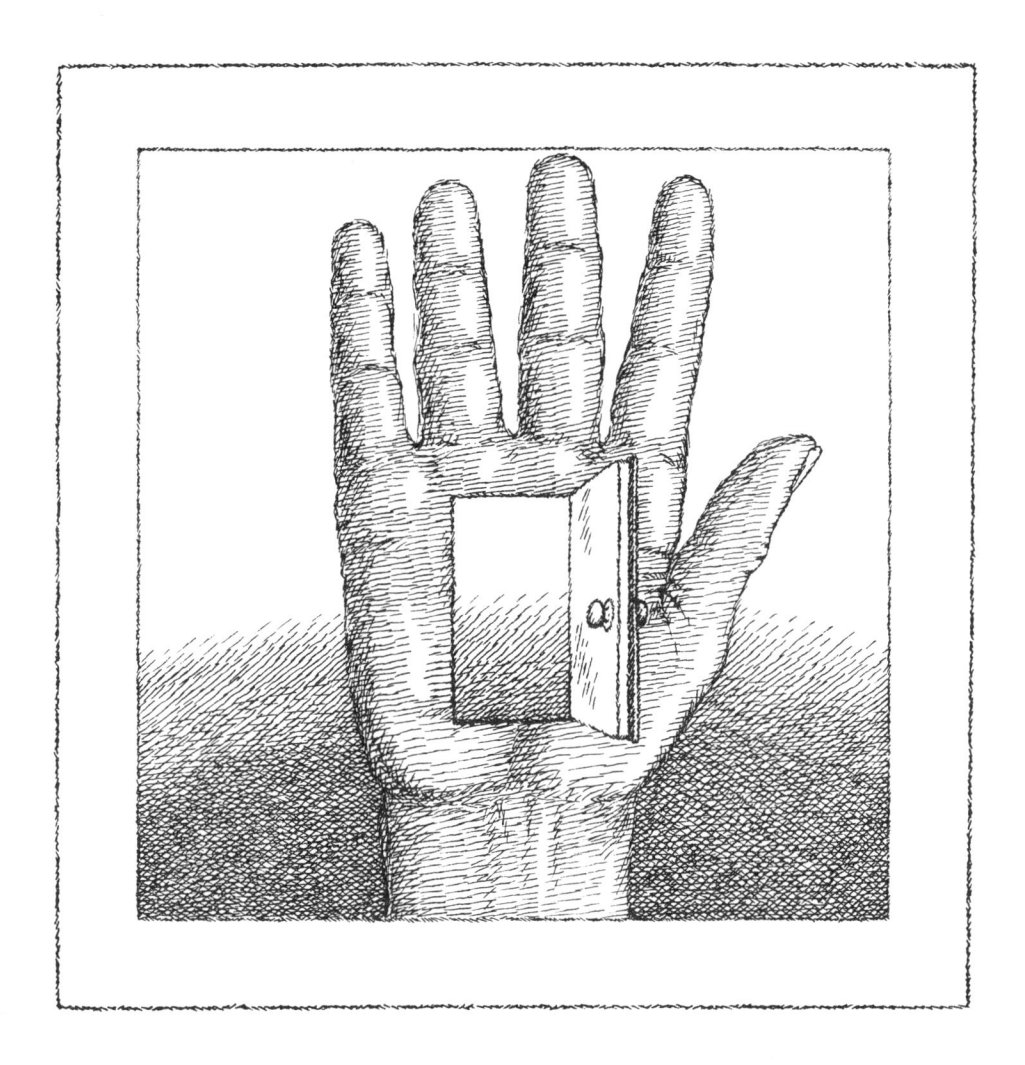

Each year half a million teenagers in the United States become mothers. The negative consequences associated with teenage parenthood have been extensively documented, and among the most profound is a greater likelihood of chronic economic insecurity and poverty. Regardless of their marital status, teenage mothers and their children are at a distinct disadvantage compared with mothers who defer childbearing and their offspring. A sixth of all American children are born to adolescent mothers. The consequences for them and for society as a whole are serious.

Given the risks and costs associated with adolescent childbearing, it is imperative that we pursue policy reforms and programmatic innovations that can improve the life chances of teenage mothers and their children. *Because schools are central to the lives of teenagers, educational institutions are critical to any effort to expand the opportunities available to student mothers.* We must ensure equitable treatment for student mothers by altering those traditional school practices that discourage them from completing high school and pursuing appropriate employment preparation. At the same time, any policy changes we pursue or programs we develop must take into consideration the needs of young children as well as the needs of their teenage mothers.

Among the obstacles that keep young mothers from continuing school, lack of affordable, acceptable child care options is critical. Most young mothers rely on private arrangements for child care since the United States does not have an adequate system of public child care assistance for mothers in school or at work. A significant proportion of teenage mothers, however, do not have the financial resources, an unemployed relative who is willing and able to care for a baby, or the management skills necessary to secure appropriate help with child care. As a result, too many young mothers remain out of school after they deliver. Because young mothers with low educational expectations are likely to experience additional unplanned pregnancies, dropping out of school has far-reaching negative consequences. Limited educational achievement and reduced employment prospects are merely the immediate effects of school dropout.

School-based child care programs have been increasingly cited as an important resource for student mothers. Such programs are a positive way to encourage young mothers to:

- return to or stay in school;
- prepare for employment;
- acquire accurate information about child development and appropriate parenting practices;
- use adult guidance appropriately on matters related to managing one's life as a mother—for example, the need to plan subsequent children; and
- practice handling separation issues with their children.

Schools and school systems that are concerned about the rights and needs of young mothers should carefully evaluate the feasibility of establishing a school-based child care center. Without such a program, many young mothers will not maintain a connection with school. Furthermore, staff at such centers are often the most energetic in pursuing the school reforms necessary to support the presence of teen mothers; they will address and help alter routine school policies and practices that adversely affect young mothers at school.

The rationale for school-based child care centers is clear: Providing such a center is an effective way to encourage school completion among student mothers; in addition, this type of program can serve as a base from which staff can develop a strategy and specific proposals to remove impediments limiting the educational options of teen mothers. Nevertheless, this approach may be interpreted as rewarding the very condition most of us do not want to foster—teenage parenthood. Therefore, school-based child care centers can be controversial.

School-based child care, however, is likely to attract widespread support for two reasons. First, the educational neglect of young mothers is costly in human and economic terms. There is substantial support for the practical notion that encouraging school participation and completion will decrease the need for more expensive and complicated interventions with these same young mothers or their children at a later point. Second, equal access to education is widely regarded as an essential right for all American youth. Title IX of the federal Educational Amendments of 1972, furthermore, offers legal support for this right with regard to women.

Title IX prohibits overt discrimination, such as exclusionary policies and practices, but also addresses a second, more subtle form of discrimination that occurs when customary school policies and practices that appear to be fair have a disproportionate impact on one sex or a segment thereof. The problems young mothers face in schools are an illustration of this second sort of discrimination. The ordinary treatment accorded students in school poses formidable barriers to school enrollment for student mothers. Inflexible attendance requirements, for example, force many young mothers to remain at home.

An interest in school-based child care for teen mothers can be grounded in a commitment to equity for women, a desire to pursue common sense with regard to young mothers, and a number of other worthy concerns, such as a belief in the positive effects of center-based care on the children of adolescent mothers. Regardless of your specific interests, we believe this handbook will be very useful.

A basic resource for people who are considering the need for and feasibility of a school-based child care program for student parents in their community, *In School Together* is divided into twelve additional chapters. The order of the chapters enables the reader-as-program-planner to follow a logical sequence of information about program development. Chapters two through twelve each cover in great detail a particular set of issues that must be addressed in creating a successful program. These chapters include advice from people who have organized and operated such centers. They cover such topics as how to assess need, how to locate and use community resources, and how to organize support. The handbook explores the many elements of program design for both the teenage mothers and their children, and it addresses the important question of how to get funded. It covers the practical matters of securing staff, finding space and what it should look like, meeting licensing requirements, and resolving management issues. The last chapter provides an extensive list of books, periodicals, and organizations that can be consulted for further information on program development and implementation.

As teenage mothers are usually the primary parent for their children and often the custodial parent as well, the handbook focuses on the needs of young mothers. Nonetheless, school-based child care programs are well-suited to assist student fathers. Many programs can and do serve teenage mothers *and* fathers.

In developing this handbook, AED staff conducted a thorough survey of program philosophy and delivery arrangements at many school-based child care programs throughout the United States. Although each center has a unique history, design, and operation, there were sufficient similarities to allow us to organize our observations into the many suggestions for how to proceed that you will find in this book.

The six sites that were selected for intensive investigations are discussed at length throughout the handbook. They were chosen because together they represent a diversity of settings and approaches. Furthermore, each program is an example of a center with highly professional staff who provided carefully tailored services for the young parents and appropriate care for their children.

We visited each site to conduct in-depth interviews with the key participants—the motivators, the innovators, the strategists, the program planners, the care givers, and the student parents. We wanted to know how the center had begun, how it had gained acceptance in the school community, and how it had become a quality program. Our informants shared their struggles, successes, mistakes, and lessons. In addition, we observed daily operations and reviewed program documents to cull useful items for inclusion in this book.

Perhaps most moving to us were stories from the teenage parents. They told us of the impact the child care center had had on their lives. Most would not have been in school without it.

Individuals or groups interested in developing a school-based child care program will face many rough moments. Many aspects of planning, design, and operation are potential trouble spots. This handbook offers the strategies and suggestions of people who surmounted such hurdles and established centers.

Ultimately the success of a school-based child care program will be evaluated by its impact on the lives of those it serves: the young mothers and their children. To serve young mothers well, it is absolutely essential to understand the nature of their difficulties. The publicity surrounding teenage mothers usually suggests that most of their problems stem from their decision to have a baby too soon. The facts are more complex.

The age at which a woman bears a child does have an independent—and in the case of teenage mothers, a negative—effect on her future well-being. But for teenage mothers, the attention paid to age often obscures the importance of other factors.

A disproportionate number of teenage mothers are from low income families. Many of the problems young mothers experience are rooted in the economic and social hardships suffered by them and their families.

Similarly a portion of the problems that plague young mothers can be attributed to the unique burdens borne by female parents today. Girls continue to be poorly prepared for economic independence because they are still treated as if marriage and motherhood were their primary vocation. Yet most mothers make substantial contributions to the financial support of their families—indeed, a significant and growing number of mothers provide the sole financial support for their families. At the same time, these mothers are expected to meet nearly all the demands of child-rearing. When the constraints imposed by inadequate preparation for work are coupled with the constraints imposed by parental obligations, a mother's capacity to compete in the labor market and to secure wages sufficient for maintaining a family is severely diminished.

Having a child as a teenager intensifies these problems. First, teenage parenthood interrupts and distorts the usual sequence of events pursued by young women in the process of growing up. Second, the problems teenage mothers encounter on account of being female, and often poor, are compounded by the deficiencies in experience characteristic of youth.

To provide appropriate services and assistance to young mothers, you will want to base your program on the facts and not the myths about young mothers. This is your first major task as a program planner—to make a case for a school-based child care center that is based on facts and to convince others that your case is compelling. The next chapter pursues this task in greater detail.

CHAPTER TWO

Need

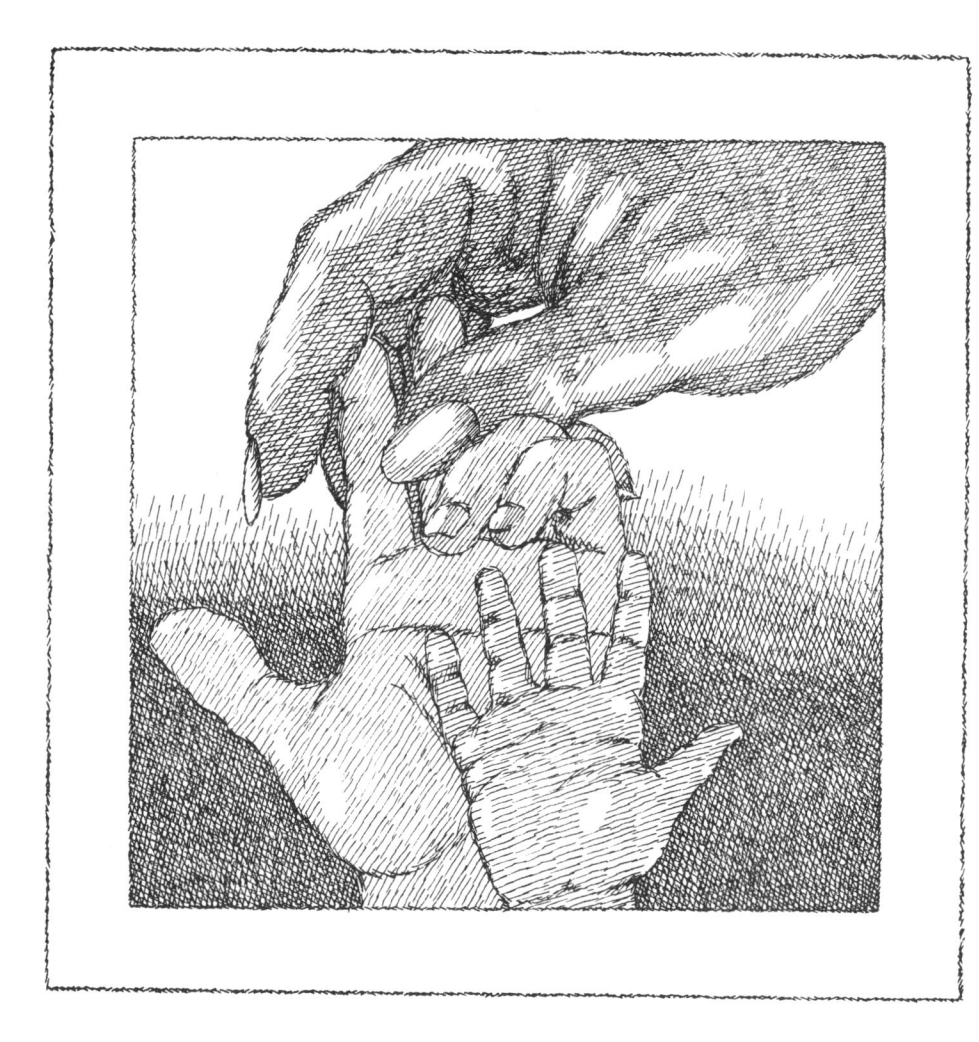

Knowledge of the facts about teenage pregnancy and parenthood is critical to getting a child care center off the ground. Teenage parenting is common. The problems associated with teenage parenting adversely affect the health of infants and the well-being of children, contribute to cycles of poverty and dependency for mothers, and exact a toll from society.

Consider these statements—all true!
- In the United States nearly half a million infants will be born this year to mothers under twenty. A majority of these mothers are still school-age.
- Teenage pregnancy and parenthood occur disproportionately among young women who are from families with low or modest incomes and who have not been successful at school work.
- Four out of ten females who are fourteen years old now will get pregnant before they are out of their teens. Half of these young women will continue their pregnancies to term.

- Most young mothers are choosing to keep and raise their children rather than seek adoptions.
- The majority of teenage mothers are not married. Those who are married are very likely to be divorced while they still have children at home. Most teenage mothers will spend some years as a single parent.
- Half of all families on welfare are headed by women who had their first child in their teens.
- Children of teenage mothers are more likely to experience a wide variety of physical, social, and developmental problems than will children born to older mothers.
- A substantial proportion of young mothers become pregnant again within two years of their first birth.
- Early parenting keeps a significant proportion of young mothers from completing high school with their peers. Yet adequate basic academic skills and a high school diploma are a critical step on the path to stronger earning power and financial independence for young mothers.
- Lack of suitable child care is cited as a major cause of absenteeism and dropout among student mothers. The dilemma of locating affordable, acceptable child care arrangements coupled with the challenge of managing school and motherhood can be overwhelmingly difficult for many mothers.

Facts such as those listed above can be powerful in the hands of someone who knows how to construct a convincing argument. They point to the straightforward argument that assisting student mothers with child care is central to helping them return to school to acquire academic and career skills. Another convincing reason to assist school age mothers with child care is to provide a mechanism whereby they can encounter sensitive, caring, skillful adults to help them manage the multiple demands they face as parents, students, and adolescents.

Establishing the need for school-based child care
There is an increasing awareness that public schools must become involved in the problems of young mothers. The personal and societal stakes are too high for them to be ignored. Schools pay in terms of high dropout rates and absenteeism. Furthermore, the children of teenage mothers pose additional problems for schools when they become students. Communities pay in terms of declining literacy and productivity. Governments, both state and federal, must pay to provide assistance for citizens who lack the education to enter the work force. To lessen these expenses, more public schools are shouldering the responsibility for helping their students cope with the problems posed by parenting. From this perspective, supporting child care services is part of the school's obligation to the community as well as to its students.

Reducing the institutional barriers that hamper young mothers at school also makes sense in terms of ensuring educational equity for all students. School systems are increasingly sensitive to the relationship between inflexible or ineffective policies and practices and school dropout. Therefore, many educators are open to new ways of meeting students' needs as well as guaranteeing students' rights.

Child care assistance offered in a school setting has many advantages for student mothers:
- On-site child care encourages mothers to stay in school. A child care program indicates a school's interest in having and helping young mothers. The program offers a base of support and assistance to mothers as well as children.

- The disruptions of adapting to new teachers, class work, and peers caused when mothers leave their home schools are avoided.
- School-based child care centers keep mothers and their babies in close proximity while mothers continue their regular studies. Schedules can be adjusted to encourage mother-child interaction throughout the day.
- Incorporating a center into a high school's administrative structure tends to ensure quality care for the children because of the school's supervisory relationship to the center.
- Transportation time and costs are cut.
- Center staff tend to take leadership roles as advocates at school and in the community for the needs and rights of student parents.

Persuading others that a school-based child care program is a good idea will take time. The foundation for success must be developed by making a compelling case that your community needs such an approach.

Documenting need

National and state context

Arguments that build from general observations to specific details are the most effective. For convenience, the facts that must be collected on adolescent parenting can be divided into three levels of focus: national, state, and local. Each level is useful for its own set of purposes and supports the next level by providing context. For example, national studies show clear links among adolescent parenting, poverty, welfare dependency, and high school dropout. Because these connections have been demonstrated nationally, there is little reason to doubt that the same is true for any and all states or communities. National statistics provide the broadest base for understanding the depth and severity of social and economic trends that touch everyone in our society. They provide a gauge by which to compare state figures, which may fall above or below national averages. Since every community is influenced by the economic and social forces at work around it, facts and statistics at the state level provide yet another point for comparison as you investigate your local situation.

"Do your homework," insist the staff of Polytechnic Child Care Center in Fort Worth, Texas. If you feel there is a need in your community for a child care center, you can begin to plan a program to address that need. Planning begins with research.

Learn everything you can about the subject, starting with national studies and statistics and working down to the local level. National and state facts are compiled, packaged, and readily available from a variety of agencies and governmental offices. A list of these resource organizations is included in Chapter 13.

For national data start with the publications of the Alan Guttmacher Institute or the Children's Defense Fund. For state data, contact both of these organizations and your state health and education departments. For local data, contact city or county public agencies, Planned Parenthood affiliates, public schools, local hospitals, and appropriate civic groups.

National and state summaries, however, stop short of the desired result because they are not personal enough. Massive numbers and generalizations are often perceived as abstract, diffuse, and unrelated to the daily affairs of most people. They lack impact. Certainly, many will acknowledge that there is a *need*. The tendency is to think that "someone" should be doing "something" about providing services to all these hundreds of thousands of mothers and infants. Yet, rarely will a barrage of facts and figures, seemingly so abstract, motivate an individual to ask what he or she can do about teen parenting in the local community.

Need in the local community

The critical questions to answer are: How does all this affect our community? Our neighborhood? Our schools? These questions require a more pointed set of answers, which will accurately describe the numbers and needs of young mothers and children who live in a particular area.

Facts on a local level cannot only convince us—as informed citizens—that the problems of adolescent parenting are *ours*, that the "someones" who could be doing something are *us,* but also motivate us to explore what exactly the "something" might be. National and state facts provide the foundation, but local facts get things done, because they describe a level of effort where individuals make a difference.

Sources for local facts

Sources at the local level vary from community to community. The amount of work you will need to do will depend on the amount of interest the subject has already attracted. Often, those who are concerned about teenage parenting in the community are a small group of people who already know each other. To determine how much information on teenage pregnancy is available in your community, contact one or more of these people.

The staff at the centers we visited reported that they identified and documented the need for a center in their respective communities by working with other staff at existing agencies or programs serving some aspect of the needs of pregnant and parenting teens. All of these professionals were concerned with determining the exact nature of the problems facing student mothers, where the need was strongest in the community, and how it might best be served. They had a personal investment in supporting a program that might extend services into a neglected area of need or an underserviced area of the community. Among them were school social workers; doctors and nurses; hospital staff and administrators; school counselors and teachers; school administrators and principals; and staff at county and city departments of child welfare, family services, health, or other branches of public welfare. Important contacts also included clergy and church groups active in community welfare and private agencies, such as United Way, the YWCA, Planned Parenthood, or other youth-serving agencies.

Remember that it is not enough to collect facts about the problem. Facts must be selected with an eye to selling the idea of a school-based child care center to those whose support is needed for it to succeed.

Essential questions and answers

National and state facts are readily available, often enough to bury a desk in stacks of summaries and reports. Local facts—*the motivators*—are harder to track down, and this requires getting answers to very specific questions. Program planners will usually have to pursue answers from firsthand sources, using the telephone and their own two feet. Bring along a notebook and enter every potential lead. These can be followed up by telephone or, whenever possible, by face-to-face interviews. The information network thus expands as each contact suggests further contacts and sources. Experience has shown that the very persons who are most knowledgeable about the subject are likely to be those that will later become staunch supporters.

Through networking, you are certain to discover like-minded allies. Therefore, it is important to be forthright about your intentions and to establish personal and personable contact.

Planners will use the results of this research in at least four different ways:
- to increase community awareness of the problems associated with adolescent parenting;
- to recruit support for a program to address the needs of young mothers and their infants;
- to convince skeptics that such a program design is both necessary and worthy of their support; and
- to convince funding sources that the program deserves financial support.

With these purposes in mind, what kinds of facts on the local level do you need? Each of the child care centers that we visited generated a different mix of what were considered essential statistics. Approaches may vary. However, for the purposes of constructing a logical argument for school-based child care services, your questions should elicit responses in three basic areas: community need, costs to the community, and the extent of services currently provided in the community. What follows is a suggested range of questions to ask local sources.

Community need. Planners are interested in measuring the occurence of teen pregnancy and parenting in the community for purposes of comparison and to pin down in numbers what is vaguely referred to as "need." How many teenage females are in the population? How many adolescent pregnancies occur every year? How many pregnancies are carried to term? What percentage of teenage pregnancies occur to school-age mothers? What percent of teenage births occur to unmarried mothers? How many births to teenage mothers are second- or higher-order births? How many school-age mothers are out of school? What proportion dropped out before they became pregnant? During pregnancy? After delivery? How many teenage mothers delivering at local hospitals or using community well-baby services do not have a high school diploma? Or adequate credentials for working? Or financial independence? Answers to these questions or variations thereof provide a standard by which the extent of community need may be conceptualized.

Costs. Planners are also interested in documenting the social and economic costs of teenage pregnancy and parenting to the community. How many infants of teenage mothers are born premature and require special hospital care? What are the costs of neonatal intensive care? What other health problems are associated with infants and mothers? Who bears the cost? How many mothers live below the poverty line? How many depend on Aid to Families with Dependent Children (AFDC) and related programs, such as Women, Infants, and Children Supplemental Feeding Program (WIC), Medicare, Medicaid, and subsidized housing? Can local dropout and absenteeism rates be correlated with pregnancy and parenting?

Community resources. Planners should survey available community resources aimed at addressing the needs of adolescent mothers and their childen to determine both what is being done and what is *not* being done. What groups or organizations regularly serve teen parents? Who sponsors special pregnancy or parenting assistance programs in the community? What kinds of programs are these? What services are offered? Are there alternative schools or facilities for pregnant students? Do they also aid these students once they become mothers? Where are facilities located?

How many teenage mothers and children are served through existing programs? What are user costs in terms of time and money? If teenage mothers are not using existing services, why not? What sorts of assistance do service providers report their teenage parent clients need? What do teenage parents report?

Sources of information on adolescent pregnancy and parenting

National
The Academy for Educational Development, School Services Division
The Alan Guttmacher Institute
The Center for Population Options
The Children's Defense Fund

State
The Alan Guttmacher Institute
The Children's Defense Fund
state health and education departments

Local
Planned Parenthood offices
U.S. Department of Health, National Center for Health Statistics, Natality Division
city and county health departments
local hospitals
public schools

See Chapter 13 for addresses, telephone numbers, and additional resources.

Surveying community resources

In each of the centers that we visited, identification and documentation of local need led to efforts to create a school-based child care center. In several cases, the gap between recognized need and the community resources available to meet it was so wide that the need for more services was considered obvious.

Answers to questions about need will allow the planners to zero in on target individuals, those in the community who could best be served by an envisioned child care center. For example, an extensive program already in place in St. Louis was designed to help teen mothers, but staff members found temporary child care facilities were needed to provide assistance while Missouri Family Services processed the mother's application for child care aid. The Crib Infant Care Center began by filling this need.

In both Elizabeth, New Jersey, and Fort Worth, Texas, the school system operated separate schools for pregnant students but did not provide any services after the birth of the child, nor did it facilitate reentry into regular high school. Most young mothers were dropping out. Thus, the idea to provide school-based infant and toddler care gained momentum.

It is possible that an informal survey of need and existing resources in the community is all that will be necessary to convince everyone involved of the need for school-based child care. However, often vital pieces of the factual puzzle are missing. High schools may not know how many students are dropping out or why. Total numbers of pregnancies and births might be fragmented across the records of various service agencies.

Tracking down the elusive gaps in records requires persistent telephone calls and footwork, a congenial manner that won't take no for an answer, and a strong measure of simple curiosity. If large gaps in needed information still seem apparent, you should consider shifting from an informal networking approach to a more formal approach.

The formal needs assessment

A formal needs assessment is a structured survey administered directly to those populations likely to use the services you are proposing or to service providers involved with your target population. Your survey may be conducted at the community, school district, neighborhood, service agency, or individual high school levels.

Of our sites, only planners in Knoxville and Fort Worth conducted a formal assessment to further pin down high school community numbers and needs. However, other centers agreed that a detailed survey would have saved everyone time, energy, and frustration, and that it might have shortened the time between idea and implementation. One informant went so far as to say that "an accurate, detailed survey of needs in the community would virtually ensure the success of a program." It should, at the least, ensure an audience for a program proposal.

For example, in 1982, the United Way of Fort Worth commissioned a comprehensive human needs survey for the city, which included sections on child care needs and adolescent pregnancy. "We discovered," said a center staff representative, "that Fort Worth was one of the communities leading the nation in teenage pregnancy." The publicized results of this survey aroused a great deal of pressure among civic groups and influential citizens for a program to meet the needs of Fort Worth's young mothers. In fact, said another center staff member, "the results of the survey were the *deciding factor* in establishing a day care center targeting student mothers."

A sponsored survey

Convincing an agency or foundation to commission a formal needs assessment can be a useful alternative to attempting one from scratch. Perhaps a local agency or foundation has already conducted a recent survey on a related topic, containing information that can be used. A telephone survey of likely organizations may bring useful statistics to light. If not, find out what resources these organizations have set aside for fact-finding activities and visit the person in charge of allocating those resources. Open up your notebook. Lay out the facts already gathered. Describe the information you are looking for. Explain your intentions. Your goals may match theirs.

This same approach might be used to convince a school board or a local high school principal to sponsor a needs assessment that would serve their interests in various ways. If records on dropout rates and reasons are incomplete, you can point to the need for the school to supply better information to the community and to the district's need for better statistics to assist planning. If dropout and absenteeism rates are particularly high, use this as evidence that schools are not responding adequately to community need. A school board may respond, if a child care planner can provide evidence that the community is interested in the local extent of teenage pregnancy and parenting problems and their effect on the schools.

Universities and community colleges have also shown interest in sponsoring such research. Colleges have experts in survey methodology and often have funds budgeted for community service activities.

Individual approaches

A planner who receives encouraging words, apologies, and little else should not despair. It is possible to do a formal needs assessment without professional help, as Lyn Overholt demonstrated at Rule High School in Knoxville, Tennessee. Assisted by a school counselor and supported by the high school principal, she conducted a written survey of all students in the school, asking about their interest in taking a laboratory course in child care. Blended into the survey were questions eliciting the number of students with children, mothers' and children's ages, and mothers' interest in using a school-based child care center.

The survey indicated that 183 students in the high school were interested in learning about child care through "hands-on" experience and that forty of these students had children eligible to participate in such a program. The school had significant absenteeism and dropout rates, which could be correlated to pregnant and parenting students. Then by using citywide statistics indicating that one out of twelve teenagers between the ages of 12 and 15 becomes pregnant, Lyn Overholt projected sobering totals for the school district. Although schools did not keep records on numbers of pregnant students or those with children, by comparing figures from social welfare and community medical sources, she was able to estimate that Rule High School had the second-highest rate from among the district's eight high schools. This combination of facts and statistics convinced many influential people in Knoxville, including district administrators and education policymakers, that the high school needed a special child care program to meet the needs of these students and their children.

Survey characteristics and administration

A formal survey should be brief and to the point, a simple questionnaire designed to measure the need for child care. Although circumstances and purposes vary, it should probably request the following information:

- ☐ age of student mother;
- ☐ grade level of student mother;
- ☐ number of children;
- ☐ ages of children;
- ☐ current child care arrangements;
- ☐ cost of arrangements;
- ☐ difficulties with arrangements; and
- ☐ interest in using school-based child care.

Getting the student to take the time to fill out a questionnaire may be more difficult than arranging to administer it. There are several ways to achieve cooperation. Lyn Overholt and her colleague surveyed the entire student population, using selected courses. Teachers directed the process and were there to answer any questions that the students had. Another approach suggested was to direct the questionnaire only to student mothers (where such information is available), using high school counselors or social workers familiar with the students and their needs. Meetings were arranged for small groups of mothers, the purpose of the survey explained, and assistance given. This approach required the cooperation of the high school principal and other school administrators.

Surveys have also been administered through health and social service programs by professionals who are already involved in providing some services to the target population. Such a survey is a critical supplement to a school survey because many school-age mothers are not in school. This approach has proven more effective in smaller communities, where the services offered and those who use them are more clearly limited.

Whatever the approach, a meaningful response to the survey—in numbers and substance—will require method, personal attention, and supervision. Educators and social services professionals can provide advice on proper survey methodology and assist in survey design.

The results of a formal needs assessment define who is in need and who will be served. School data on the number of students who drop out or have serious attendance problems provides a focus on where services should be provided. Documentation of insufficient community services suggests why a school-based child care center is necessary. These are the enlightening facts, the ones that bring concerned individuals face to face with an awareness of community responsibility, that motivate them and convince others that action is not only possible but necessary.

Packaging information

The final task of research is to summarize, in written form, the evidence that has been gathered. The resulting document should repeat the steps of research, that is, provide a national and state context for locally generated facts, and present them in a logical fashion. Solid information will generally speak for itself and decrease the need for purely emotional appeals. However, carefully selected anecdotes that drive home the need for the service you are proposing are often effective and are not out of place. "Real life" stories allow the reader to identify with young mothers on a personal level. For example, planners at one site described a single individual's struggle to stay in school—the difficulty of arranging dependable child care, how it conflicted with attending school, and how it created stress for her and her infant.

Depending on their resources and sponsors, the programs we surveyed produced a variety of research documents. The slickest were printed pamphlets, produced as a comprehensive community study. However, other planners presented their results by typing and photocopying. Format is less important than content.

The resulting document provides a convenient focus for subsequent publicity and advocacy efforts. It can be used to interest local newspaper editors in running an article or series of articles on the problems of teenage pregnancy and parenting in the community. Often initial publicity of this sort is needed to bring the issues before the public and to legitimize public discussion. The document may be used to approach local organizations, clubs, and churches for their support. These groups may welcome a speaker on the subject of adolescent pregnancy and parenting. These approaches contribute to the community's awareness and provide a general climate of support for programs.

The document can also be used as a vehicle to present the need for school-based child care to the school board, school administrators, and high school principals. It provides a concrete focus for discussion and debate. Presenting information before the school board can provide an opportunity to test the political climate, to determine which policymakers are informed on the subject, which seem receptive, and which seem likely to support any proposals generated through the planning process.

These are initial steps. However, more specific support often needs to be organized. A clear and concise research document can be used to focus discussion, elicit interest, and attract allies. The next chapter discusses ways to bring together concerned professionals and influential community citizens to act as advocates for school-based child care and to design a program to meet the community needs that research has revealed.

CHAPTER THREE

Support Strategies

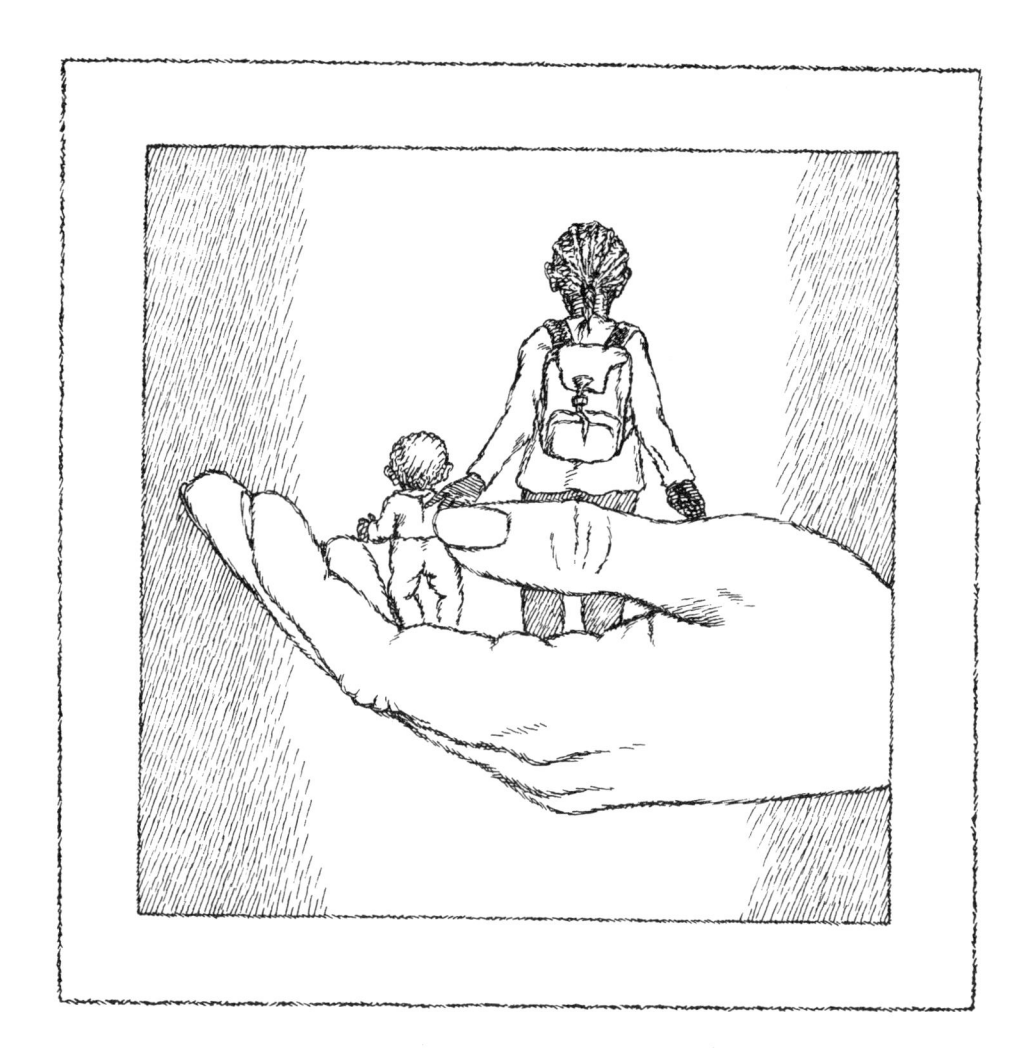

Organizing support is an ongoing task. It begins with the first steps of finding allies committed to program development and extends through program operations. The histories of the child care centers we surveyed indicate that approaches to organizing support varied but that initiators in every city spent much time and effort building support for the centers. This support then ensured the establishment of the center and was a continuing resource to strengthen the programs offered. Support begins with committed individuals and includes the basic building blocks of an advocacy committee—drawn from social services, health, and education activists—and an advisory board, which extends membership to policymakers and community leaders.

Where community interest is high and resources available, an advisory board often precedes and subsumes the advocacy committee. Otherwise, an advocacy committee is formed from participants in the informal information network and works to broaden its base of support by creating an advisory board. The choice of one strategy over the other will depend on the amount and type of groundwork already laid in the community.

The advocacy committee

Information gathering will have brought you into direct contact with a group of interested or actively involved professionals (and, in some instances, volunteers). Some will have been very helpful, sharing contacts and suggestions, offering anecdotes that vividly describe need in the community, or providing the important local data that you have summarized. These people comprise a powerful network and, according to our respondents, can become the core of support for any school or community program targeting adolescent mothers. They have the collective community experience and persuasiveness to advise community policymakers. Their combination of skills and positions makes them the most successful advocates of school-based child care in any community.

Often a single, well-placed individual committed to your issue can accomplish much. More often, however, successful programs were built by a group of concerned individuals organizing themselves as a committee or task force around the issue of adolescent pregnancy. Their goals were to publicize community need and to develop specific recommendations for school and community response. A formal group with these objectives can be convened from among members of your informal network as easily as surveying contacts by telephone and setting a date for a meeting of those interested. The most difficult task will probably be finding a time that fits with everyone's busy schedule. A committee convened in this way proceeds by established rules of order, electing a chairperson, deciding on an agenda, and moving on the business at hand.

The struggle to implement school-based child care is typically fought in a small arena. Although some degree of community awareness and involvement is considered essential, political mobilization of broad segments of the community is usually not needed. Most centers we surveyed began with a few individuals who galvanized the interest and support of others. These individuals identified the problem from a variety of perspectives. They included: a community social worker, a high school principal, a foundation officer, a central school district administrator, two teachers, and a volunteer. Once organized, these activists persuaded community officials, school board members, district administrators, and high school principals, that child care services were necessary and would serve the broader needs of the community.

Child care advocates often seek out a local agency, foundation, or other type of organization that is willing to sponsor an adolescent parents advocacy committee. In several communities, publicity was effective enough or interest strong enough, to impel school board or community officials to sponsor a committee to conduct further research or to offer recommendations for specific interventions. Sponsors were usually willing to delegate far-reaching responsibilities to a committee's members, allowing them to play a pivotal role in designing and implementing programs.

The purpose of an advocacy committee is to persuade those who have the power to approve or veto any program that goes into the schools (that is, district superintendents, school board members, and high school prinicipals) that services are needed to effectively educate a portion of the teenage population. These are the people to convince, and they should be the particular target of any information program or lobbying that a committee decides to undertake.

Most school administrators are under serious time as well as fiscal constraints. They often do not have access to concrete local data, firsthand observations and anecdotes, or other specific evidence that documents the role child care plays in supporting children and getting mothers through school. The advocacy committee should take steps to supply that information in a concise and logical manner. Presenting documentation can capture the attention of policymakers, engender trust, and build credibility.

Rule High School planners compiled the costs for one mother and one baby on public assistance from the baby's birth until the mother reached the age of eighteen. They stressed that the younger a mother is when first giving birth, the greater the likelihood of her having more children before the age of twenty, thus multiplying the costs. They then discussed these figures with school administrators, emphasizing the cost-effectiveness of a child care center that teaches parenting skills and ways to prevent repeat pregnancies. This proved to be a persuasive strategy.

Community resources for support

Child care and youth-serving agencies
Girls Club of America
YWCA and YMCA
child study centers
jobs for youth projects
local youth service collaborations
teenage pregnancy networks

City, county, and state government agencies
adolescent pregnancy study or policy committees
child welfare
health department
human resources department
programs for children with developmental disabilities
public welfare
youth and family services

Civic and community organizations
Junior League
United Way
Urban League
fraternal organizations

Foundations and trusts
community trusts
local foundations

Health and medical resources
Planned Parenthood
Red Cross
community health centers
hospitals: adolescent health and obstetrics and gynecology divisions
insurance companies: health maintenance division
medical schools
medical societies
mental health associations
nursing schools
nutrition programs
visiting nurses associations

Religious organizations
Catholic charities
Jewish family and children's services
ecumenical societies and action committees
local churches

School-based resources
Parent–Teacher Association
departments of attendance, guidance, health, pupil personnel, and vocational education
school nurses
schools for pregnant students

Strategies for winning support

As a first step, an advocacy committee must push for a consensus that something needs to be done. In addition, the committee must focus on defining an adequate intervention by or within the school system to assist young mothers. Finally, the committee must prove that there is the kind of community support needed to justify the school district's involvement in child care. Researching, networking, and organizing are the principal tools of the advocacy committee for accomplishing the tasks that face them.

Each child care center that was visited generated support in different ways, suggesting a range of possible strategies. The right strategy needs to be shaped by the advocates' understanding of the mix of persons, resources, community attitudes, and local political climate. The following stories from six school-based centers demonstrate that building support among policymakers requires flexibility, persistence, and political savvy.

Crib Infant Care Center

The Crib Infant Care Center of Vashon High School, St. Louis, Missouri, began through the efforts of a well-placed professional who recognized the need for assistance to young mothers. Jane Paine, working through the St. Louis-based Danforth Foundation, was instrumental in bringing together a committee of education, health care, and social service professionals to study the city's adolescent pregnancy and parenting problems. Under the aegis of the Danforth Foundation this group was empowered to:

- study and document the problem;
- study the need for education on family life and parenting;
- develop the outline for school-based programs to meet these needs;
- identify schools with the highest incidence of pregnancy and parenting; and
- design a pilot program and secure funding for it.

The committee's work to meet these objectives led to development of the Parent/Infant Interaction Program (PIIP), a comprehensive pilot project funded by the Danforth Foundation and the Charles Stewart Mott Foundation. Until PIIP, a single alternative school served pregnant students citywide, about 360 each year. PIIP's goal was to provide better and more available services to an estimated two thousand adolescent parents, both in and out of school. PIIP began operations in August, 1978, under the auspices of the Continued Education Division of the St. Louis Public Schools and was situated at two community schools that had high birth rates among adolescents.

The next step involved leadership by a school principal, Michael Thomas of Vashon High School. After two years of PIIP operations elsewhere, Thomas began a community education program in his school designed to use the school as a resource center for the community. Part of Thomas's plan included centering PIIP at Vashon, with five satellites across the city at community schools, neighborhood health clinics, and high schools.

PIIP staff had identified infant care to be the largest problem in helping young mothers to stay in school, and child care services for student mothers fit well with Thomas's concepts. Through PIIP and a planning committee, once again brought together by Jane Paine, he arranged to start the Crib Infant Care Center at Vashon. Community response was so favorable that all of PIIP's operations were incorporated in the high school's budget under Vashon Youth Support Services. The program is now autonomous. It operates in Vashon High School, but it is not directly supervised by the principal.

In St. Louis, the gap between need and services appeared very wide. With strong foundation support, Jane Paine was able to organize an ambitious committee to study the problem. Michael Thomas was designing improvements in his school to prevent school dropout. He recognized the need for child care services for student mothers and tapped the PIIP resource network that was already in place. Joining PIIP and school resources under the umbrella of Vashon Youth Support Services enabled child care and other PIIP services to spread to other schools in the city. For St. Louis, it was a highly successful combination.

Center for Infant Development

The Center for Infant Development in Elizabeth, New Jersey, grew out of an existing program, an alternative education program aimed at pregnant students. Prior to 1973 when it became illegal, this school district's policy (similar to a majority of others in the country) was to dismiss pregnant students. In Elizabeth these students were referred to a school social worker, who located other assistance for them. The social worker, Harriet Bloomfield, recognized the need for an educational alternative to allow these young women to continue their studies, at least until they had their babies and could return to regular classes. At her insistence, student social workers from Rutgers University completed a needs assessment and recommended establishing a special classroom facility. In response, the Board of Education and the local government approved an alternative education program outside the regular school, which began operating in donated space provided by the YWCA. Eventually, the program moved to its current location in the school superintendent's building.

After several years, Harriet Bloomfield recognized that the existing program kept young women in class until they became mothers, but that most then dropped out because of insufficient child care. She submitted a proposal to the New Jersey Department of Human Services to establish a child care facility, which was funded.

To broaden her base of support, Bloomfield organized an advisory board composed of health and education professionals. She needed to gain allies who believed that providing child care for student mothers was an activity appropriate to school board involvement. This advisory board was influential in persuading the school board to act as disburser for funds. The center opened, initially housed in a mobile trailer that was not on the high school grounds. The advisory board continued to play an important role as the center became established and was critical in persuading the school board to incorporate the center more fully into its administration and to provide in-kind services for the center. At this point, city policymakers were persuaded to purchase and renovate a centrally located site that could more conveniently serve student mothers.

The alternative education program that was the springboard for child care in Elizabeth, New Jersey, grew slowly, working its way from a YWCA-donated space to its present site in the school building that also houses the superintendent's office. The Center for Infant Development began in a separate trailer facility and moved into a city-purchased space. Each move reflected growth in the programs, greater community acceptance, and further integration into the school district's permanent administrative structure. The center was the result of persistent and painstaking consensus building. The center's strong advisory board was influential in gaining the school board's support and in maintaining consensus.

Bay Ridge LYFE Program

Instead of starting a program at the periphery and gradually working into an accepted niche, Carol Burt-Beck used the administrative hierarchy to implement a program from within the system. Carol Burt-Beck worked from the New York City Board of Education's Office of Funded Programs to research the need for child care programs and to identify resources for such programs. No formal survey was taken, although available statistics suggested that over thirty thousand teen pregnancies occurred each year in the city. Through strategic networking, Carol Burt-Beck met with the head of the New York City Division of High Schools and explained her intention to initiate services for adolescent mothers. He agreed that services were necessary and brought her on to the central staff to develop an initiative program.

During this time, an Adolescent Pregnancy Task Force, composed of representatives from a wide variety of public agencies, educators, well-known advocacy experts, and community service providers, was formed by New York City Council President Carol Bellamy to support research and program development. Carol Burt-Beck was appointed to the task force as Chairperson of the Child Care Subcommittee. This position, with its influential political backing, allowed her to secure city funds to start a child care initiative. She designed and established two Living for the Young Family through Education (LYFE) child care centers, one in Harlem, the other at Bay Ridge High School in Brooklyn, aimed at low-income adolescent mothers.

The LYFE centers provide the clearest example of effective information and support networking. Carol Burt-Beck had a very clear understanding of how the New York City school system operates and was able to use her position on central staff and as a Pregnancy Task Force appointee to secure approval from essential policymakers. The LYFE programs are, indeed, a very small part of a large bureaucracy supervised by the Division of High Schools and by community school boards. In turn, these are under the jurisdiction of the New York City Board of Education, overseeing services to 960,000 students. Under these circumstances, Burt-Beck's strategy of working from the top down was admirably effective.

Polytechnic Child Care Center

The other end of the strategy spectrum might well be represented by the child care center established at Polytechnic High School, Fort Worth, Texas. The context, both in terms of the city and the school system, is less centralized, more pluralistic, and cooperative. Social services to Fort Worth youth are coordinated by a coalition, called the Tarrant County Youth Collaboration (TCYC), of over fifty local agencies and private foundations. These agencies pool information and resources to tackle social problems as a whole, rather than in pieces. Moreover, state and federal grants for programs in the city are rare, and the city government makes much of the idea that Fort Worth takes care of its own.

At the time the issue of a child care center was raised, the school district was supporting a single-site, alternative school, New Lives, which accepted students from across the city. The Superintendent of Schools and the School Board were reform oriented and actively pursued services for disadvantaged students. Despite New Lives it was discovered that teen mothers were not completing their schooling, most often because of inadequate child care.

New Lives personnel approached the United Way to furnish a social worker to address the dropout problem. In partial response, the United Way commissioned a comprehensive needs assessment, which set in motion a complex chain of events. Results of the survey were reported to the school district, which created a citizens advisory committee to study the problems of teenage pregnancy, to make recommendations, and to report to the School Board. The School Board then formally convened an Adolescent Pregnancy Advisory Committee (APAC), which was empowered:

- to hire an Adolescent Pregnancy Services Coordinator;
- to develop a comprehensive approach to meet the needs of pregnant and parenting adolescents, which was to increase community awareness, reassess the New Lives program, and create both a child care pilot program and an education pilot program; and
- to raise funds from organizations and foundations in the city to support adolescent pregnancy services.

The APAC was designed as a broadly based committee, whose members were prominent citizens, social welfare, health, and education professionals, directors and staff of local foundations, and business leaders. A subcommittee designed the child care program.

As the school district did not want to enter the child care business per se, it searched for a provider agency with prior child care experience to implement the program. The YWCA already operated one child care center and expressed interest in developing another in the vicinity of Polytechnic High School. The school board formalized a subcontracting arrangement with the YWCA, which then received city and private foundation moneys to establish a center for the high school. The arrangement was agreeable to both parties, as services could be delivered more efficiently and expediently.

Fort Worth worked from the bottom up by committee. Need was recognized by New Lives staff, documented by the United Way, and responded to by the superintendent and the school board. A formal advisory board was established with the broadest possible community representation, which sanctioned a child care program designed by its subcommittee and implemented by a private agency with both public and private foundation funding. The Polytechnic Child Care Center was but one result of an extensive collaboration aimed at providing comprehensive services for the city's pregnant and parenting adolescents. In this instance, committees, rather than single dynamic individuals, were the vehicles for action. Sources of support were broadly organized rather than narrowly defined.

Infant-Toddler Child Development Center

The Infant-Toddler Child Development Center of Murray-Wright High School, Detroit, Michigan, has an unusual history. It grew out of existing child development, child care, and home economics courses to become both a child care center and a vocational education laboratory. Prompted by requests from students in their courses, and from several student mothers with young children, Dolores Norman and Cora Eubanks—respectively, supervisor of the Vocational Education Department and supervisor of the Home Economics Department—designed a laboratory program that would include infants and toddlers to provide child care and child care training. The high school principal backed their initiative and was instrumental in gaining support from key decision makers at the district level. They organized a Vocational Advisory Committee, composed of professionals and community representatives. This committee had a tough task. A vocal minority felt that school-based child care might condone early parenting. The committee disagreed and had enough collective clout to overrule. Funded by vocational education grants, the laboratory center became a successful and highly popular high school program.

Norman, Eubanks, and the principal of Murray-Wright High School began with a site and an existing program of services and worked to expand coverage to infant care. Attracting support from outside, however, proved challenging. Implementation required overcoming a perceived indifference and lack of understanding of the problems among critical decision makers and opposition from others who objected to the center on moral grounds. The decision to locate the advocacy task with the Vocational Advisory Committee proved to be important in overcoming opposition. It broadened the support base and gained the needed approval.

Preschool/Parenting Learning Center

The Rule High School Preschool/Parenting Learning Center in Knoxville, Tennessee, also found its niche as a child care laboratory program. After observing the academic, financial, and emotional problems of teenage mothers, Lyn Overholt, a volunteer in a high school tutoring program, and Mariana Davis, a school counselor, began to discuss ways of addressing these problems. Together they outlined a program of services and began exploring ways to house the program in the high school, where services would readily be available to student mothers. They consulted with the head of the Department of Child and Family Studies at the University of Tennessee to develop a proposal for a center for children of Rule High School students. The proposed center was to provide both care for the children and training opportunities for Rule High students.

The proposal was presented to the school district's Curriculum Coordinating Committee and was approved after much discussion. Lyn Overholt and Mariana Davis then met with district administrators, who lent their support in writing a funding proposal and developing a budget. The district superintendent was also persuaded to support the proposal, which was submitted for state funding. At this point, disagreement among school board members threatened to stop the program. One member characterized the proposed program as "predicated on illegitimacy" and "a veritable quagmire of immorality." This position was backed by only one other board member, but the highly publicized rhetoric delayed a vote of support.

One respondent, however, said: "In the end, I think all the controversy helped us more than it hurt. The debate was very public, and the bulk of support came down on our side." Eventually, the center was approved.

In Knoxville, Overholt and Davis displayed admirable networking skills, drawing on university and other professional expertise, using district administrators to help sort out funding possibilities and budget realities, and lining up influential policymakers, such as the district superintendent, to promote their initiative. The heart of the effort was gaining school board approval, which was eventually secured through public debate.

The advisory board

Typically, an advisory board is a citizen's group empowered to advise administrators in decisions of policy and practice as they relate to program operations. Administrators are expected to consult with advisory board members but are not technically bound to abide by their decisions. Among the centers that were visited, however, advisory boards often played an expanded role, approaching that of a governing board or board of directors. School boards often found it useful to relegate oversight responsibilities for school-based centers to an advisory board, thus relieving school administrators of the task. Advisory board members were made answerable to the school board for any problems in the center and were expected to take steps to remedy those problems. School boards seemed content to allow free rein in terms of policy decisions, so long as these did not conflict with established school policies and so long as centers functioned smoothly. An advisory board's role may be significantly limited when funding is directly funneled through the school board. However, greater autonomy is generally considered more practical since it provides a governing body that is both immediate in attention and flexible in response.

Selecting members

A community program should be directed by citizens interested and involved in programs for infants and young children. Accepting advisory board membership is an important community responsibility, and members should be selected with care. They must oversee the correct operations of the center and represent it in any community debate, answering for questions of policy and behavior. They will need to keep informed about the program and about how it relates to other services in the community. Therefore, members should be responsive to and representative of the entire community.

Board members should be sought from all socioeconomic strata, from a range of ethnic and religious groups, from differing political stances, and from professional, business, and other interest groups that make up the community. The key is to present a broad community front of support, rather than seeming to represent the interests of a parochial group. Representatives of groups focused on women's issues, community health and social services agencies, local foundations, businesses, and social, religious, and political groups should be recruited for membership.

Boards that are either too small or too large are detrimental to effective communications and decision making. Therefore, an optimum number, one that both reflects community diversity and is still small enough to allow close relations, needs to be selected. Among centers studied, membership ranged from twelve to twenty-five persons.

Advisory board responsibilities

Advisory boards typically have three primary responsibilities:
- to establish, continually reevaluate, and modify the center's policies;
- to secure adequate financial support for the program; and
- to communicate the program's purposes, successes, and problems to the community.

To accomplish these objectives, members may be asked to:
- determine the general policies and direction of the program;
- select a person or group to design the program;
- oversee the program development and approve a budget;
- sponsor planners in locating and securing financial support;
- locate and secure space and facilities for the center;
- recruit and hire a program director;
- endorse the center's existence and operations within the community; and
- evaluate the program according to selected outcomes.

A large board may wish to divide into standing subcommittees with specific responsibility for administration, finances, personnel, health, site and space, social services liaison, planning, and so forth. A smaller advisory board may simply divide into parent/participant advisory, technical advisory, and policy advisory groups. Organizing at this level may precede or be pursued concurrently with other planning and design activities.

Identifying key sources of support

Use this form to record the organizations and representatives that can contribute to the founding of your child care center. Use check marks to delineate roles that each organization and individual might be expected to play.

organization and contact to involve	knows needs and problems	provides services to teenage parents	has needed resources	has approval power	can give support or legitimacy	has potential to undermine
child care and youth-serving						
organization						
contact						
organization						
contact						
organization						
contact						
community						
organization						
contact						
organization						
contact						
organization						
contact						
government						
organization						
contact						
organization						
contact						
organization						
contact						

organization and contact to involve	knows needs and problems	provides services to teenage parents	has needed resources	has approval power	can give support or legitimacy	has potential to undermine
foundations and trusts						
organization						
contact						
organization						
contact						
organization						
contact						
health and medical						
organization						
contact						
organization						
contact						
organization						
contact						
religious						
organization						
contact						
organization						
contact						
organization						
contact						
school-based						
organization						
contact						
organization						
contact						
organization						
contact						

Conclusions and considerations

Condensing these examples into a concise prescription for developing program support is not an easy task, nor is it necessarily desirable. Each center studied attracted a blend of advocates from a range of backgrounds and positions. Each adopted a strategy that seemed appropriate to its immediate goals and local milieu.

In most cases, a small but highly motivated advocacy committee was the driving force behind generating support for, designing, and implementing the day care center. The advocacy committee is the work horse of a child care initiative. Eventually, the advocacy committee usually worked under the sponsorship of the school district, of another community agency, or as part of a more broadly based advisory board.

Where a formal advisory board was formed, it enlarged the community base of support for programs by involing other concerned and influential citizens. Wider support provided leverage for program initiatives and hastened their approval through bureaucratic channels. In several communities where interest in the issues of adolescent pregnancy and parenting was especially high, such as Fort Worth and St. Louis, a community advisory board actually preceded the formation of an advocacy committee, more exclusively concerned with child care.

An advisory board often functioned under the sponsorship of an umbrella agency, such as a school board or a private foundation. Sponsored committees or boards appeared most effective in designing comprehensive service programs for the community, of which child care was a single component. This combination of professionals, educators, representatives of private organizations, and business leaders is especially suited to getting things done. An advisory board also proves useful in resolving conflicts of operations or management that may develop later in implementing the program.

Where a formal community-based committee group is already focusing on issues related to adolescent pregnancy in your community, consider joining forces and using the ready-made base to support child care initiatives. Even among those who are active with the issues, the need for school-based child care is not always clearly understood, or else child care is given a lower priority. Yet school-based child care may fill an essential niche in an otherwise comprehensive approach to services delivery.

In cities where interest had not previously led to organization, as in Elizabeth or Knoxville, the advocacy committee became the basic building block of support. In such cases, information projects and networking were aimed at expanding a circle of professional advocates to form a more broadly based coalition. The eventual creation of an advisory board ensured long-term community support.

The high school principal's leadership and/or support was, in many cases, decisive in beginning a child care center in a school or bringing an existing one to the school. The principal of the target high school should be recruited as an essential supporter.

Convincing school board members also becomes essential. Bringing a proposal before a school board is the most political part of the process, and any opposition is certain to emerge here. Child care planners stuck to the facts and sought to avoid emotional debate over moral issues.

Opposition

No center was formed without some form of opposition. However, in most cases, planners found that opposition to their efforts was less substantial than was initially feared or predicted. Opposition can take many forms.

In many communities, bringing child care into the schools is a potentially volatile issue. Many oppose these centers because they believe that a center will somehow encourage teenagers to have more children. It is important to marshal evidence and develop arguments to demonstrate that this is untrue.

Opponents often appeal to religious tenents to condemn premarital sex. They feel that the solution to teen parenting problems lies in instilling morality to curb sexual activity, not in providing child care. Advocates should stress that their efforts do not negate concerns about sexual morality. Child care and morality are not mutually exclusive. However, well-intentioned moral concerns do not address the immediate goals of keeping young mothers in school or assuring that children, *already born*, are provided adequate care and attention. "Services *must* be provided for these students, or you can just write them off," was the attitude of center advocates in Knoxville. "There are few moral justifications for punishing young women for becoming mothers."

Other opponents expressed concern that school-based child care was the equivalent of providing what they called free babysitting services to irresponsible mothers. This attitude was eased by stressing the positive results of assisting teens in parenting skills and by center policies that encouraged responsible parenting. (At one center, for example, some payment, according to income, was required as a means of assuring parental commitment.) Center advocates continually argue that if some mothers appear to be irresponsible, it is not by choice, but because of inexperience and lack of education.

Center planners themselves have expressed hesitation. In Detroit, advocates were concerned that child care at Murray-Wright High School would be seen as a coddling, condoning mechanism. These concerns were addressed by establishing tough guidelines that demanded responsible behavior of mothers. Where opposition is particularly strong, such guidelines can be built into the program design.

In debates over these and similar issues, the evidence that school-based child care is a successful intervention is consistently on the side of advocates. The best strategy is to stick to the facts and avoid emotional arguments. Such arguments tend to fall apart through inherent inconsistencies when confronted with a rational and factual presentation.

In spite of the best efforts of planners and advocates, there will always be those whose minds are made up and who will never be convinced of the value of school-based child care. They must simply be out-voted.

Perhaps the most pernicious form of opposition is passive. Advocates must often contend with the passivity of key decision makers, such as school officials, who may be reluctant to learn about or support a program that might seem complex or prove controversial. School board members may shy away from the whiff of controversy, that, they feel, might cost an election. The best antidote to these attitudes is to recruit advocates from a broad front, to present documentation, and to demand attention.

CHAPTER FOUR
Design

The previous chapter discussed ways to transform individual commitment into collective effort and explored strategies to organize community support. Now it is necessary to focus more closely on the practical matters of designing a school-based child care center. As Carol Burt-Beck demonstrated with the LYFE program, it *is* possible, with the right position and contacts, to launch a program more-or-less singlehandedly. However, in most cases, a group or committee will work together to plan the center.

Planning

There is no one way to design a program. An advocacy committee, advisory board, or school administration may appoint or hire an experienced individual to design a program. A planning committee may be selected to develop a program. Yet in every case, the planner or planners must pursue the following overall goals:

□ determine concrete program objectives to meet the documented needs;
□ define the scope of the program;
□ examine alternative options for programming; and
□ explore connections with school and community resources.

Determining program priorities

Purpose and objectives

Many needs deserve to be addressed, but it is important to establish program objectives that can be realistically met and that will be supported by the school and the community. The interests of possible funding sources should also be kept in mind. While it is possible to restrict objectives only to child care, all of our centers were equally concerned about educational objectives with regard to the student parents. Educational objectives were sometimes targeted at young mothers alone but in other instances they embraced fathers or nonparenting students interested in learning about child care. In addition, most centers listed objectives for the infants and toddlers served by the program.

For example, the designers of the Center for Infant Development in Elizabeth viewed their center as a "psycho-social" service for school-aged mothers. The center's main objective was to provide quality child care to "free-up" school-aged mothers to complete their education, but the center wanted to be more than just a baby-sitting facility. Specific child development and parent training goals were included. The center provided a nurturing environment, encouraged early learning experiences, and tracked individual infant development, while mothers were educated in proper nutrition, hygiene, and child development.

The LYFE center at Bay Ridge High School adopted a three-tier approach to establishing center objectives with specific goals for infants and toddlers, for mothers, and for the parent/child relationship. For infants and toddlers, objectives were to provide developmental assessment, medical/developmental information, an individualized curriculum, and social stimulation. For mothers, the center sought to provide an environment where they could learn decision making and explore life options and skills. The center also wanted to teach basic parenting skills and encourage positive mother/child interaction through care and play.

Consider how the above objectives can shape a program's design. The program director needs a strong background in child growth and development. Concise health and developmental records need to be kept. Some type of ongoing groups need to be set up for mothers to learn about life skills. Mothers need to be integrated into program operations to allow opportunities for supervised interaction, as in regularly scheduled feeding and play sessions. "Off-time" needs to be arranged with school administration so that mothers can visit their infants between classes.

Scope also varies. The Crib Infant Care Center at Vashon High School, due to the sheer numbers of young mothers, concentrated on providing high-quality, temporary child care only, providing subsequent referrals to other public and private child care facilities in the community. It operated as a transition center and was able to serve more mothers, but for a shorter time. Most other centers we surveyed offered longer-term care, allowing mothers to participate until their high school graduation. Nonetheless, scope also varied significantly among these centers.

Visiting other centers

As they entered the design process, planners found it useful to visit other child care centers. Planners from Fort Worth visited centers in Austin, El Paso, and Albuquerque, New Mexico. Bay Ridge High School planners visited the Bank Street Infant Center in New York City. Planners for the Rule High School center observed school-based centers in Washington, D.C., and the Infant and Toddler Laboratories at the University of Tennessee.

Consultations with child development specialists at local universities generated a range of program models from which to borrow. However, none of our informants adopted any single model in its entirety. Each felt that his or her particular program was unique and finely tuned to the community. Common complaints were that other models were targeted to middle and upper-middle class populations and were less suited to the needs of adolescent mothers, or the scope was too narrow or too wide. Although, under closer scrutiny, no program is truly unique, every center developed an individualized blend of objectives and components that was adapted to community needs and resources. Designers struggled in every case to make the program their own.

Choosing your objectives

What do you want your child care center to do? Given resources and the size of the target population, what can it realistically do? What follows is a list of specific objectives developed by other centers that should be useful in making a list of your own.

Providing quality services for infants/toddlers

Objectives in this area should be to:
- provide a safe, nurturing atmosphere for infants that allows close proximity and daily contact with parents;
- provide a comprehensive curriculum for young children that meets social, physical, and developmental needs;
- reduce child neglect by providing a healthy, supportive environment and by monitoring for signs of physical abuse; and
- ensure adequate, appropriate nutrition and encourage development of sound health habits under supervision of qualified personnel.

Assisting the continued education of student parents

Educational goals for parents should be to:
- assist student parents in completing their education by providing quality and affordable child care; and
- reduce the incidence of dropping out, lowered achievement, and welfare dependency by providing convenient, accessible care.

Developing students' parenting skills

To establish goals in this area, the center should:
- work directly with student parents and their infants on bonding and other positive interactions to ensure healthy development;
- teach effective verbal techniques for handling negative behavior of children;
- offer guidance in basic child rearing skills; and
- help parents face the challenges of child rearing realistically, including the need to delay further childbearing until the mother has acquired adequate credentials for working.

Involving parents with the community

Referrals were an essential part of each of the centers that were visited. Centers sought to:
- provide information about and referral to other community programs and services; and
- provide advocacy around gaining access to community resources in the areas of housing, health, and consumer affairs.

Providing vocational training for parents and nonparent students

Several centers sought to broaden the scope of their program to include laboratory or vocational objectives, such as to:
- integrate student parents into vocational training programs to improve their employability; and
- use the center as a laboratory setting to provide training for students entering child care fields.

Program scope

A concrete list of objectives is the basis for program design. Deciding on program scope is the next element in the equation.

Progam scope can be broadened or narrowed by adjusting the eligibility criteria set for children, by limiting service to mothers at specific grade levels or ages, by focusing the program exclusively on child care components, or by expanding it to include a whole range of components aimed at parents or to include nonparent students. Restricting program focus greatly simplifies design, implementation, and cost, while expanding it often builds support among policymakers and opens up different funding opportunities. The trade-offs need to be discussed. How can the program do the most good for the most participants? Where should resources be concentrated? What approach will appeal most strongly to the school board, district administrators, and high school principal? Do funding options need to be expanded? Should you start small and grow or try to do more from the first days of operation?

Planners are encouraged to plan around a single neighborhood or high school. Most of the centers we visited began with a single site. Most started with enrollments of eight to fifteen children and expanded to twenty to thirty-five children—a medium-sized center. School-based centers tend to have smaller enrollments but offer a wider range of services than other community child care centers.

Many experienced center planners advise limiting direct services in the beginning. This strategy emphasizes infant/toddler care and parenting skills components and keeps other activities to a minimum. Social services referrals may be made through school health and guidance offices. As the basic program succeeds, the educational curriculum for parents may be expanded and other services initiated.

If need in the school is particularly high, more mothers and infants may still be served by juggling the ages of infants' admission and discharge. Centers surveyed served a range of ages: from six weeks to one-and-a-half years, from two weeks to two years, or from four months to four years. Programs can also target mothers at a certain grade level, for example, giving enrollment preference to juniors and seniors. Limiting enrollment in these ways can enable a center to reach more of its target population over the course of a year.

Of course, you may have the opposite concern in your community. You may need to *attract* participants, rather than turn them away, which can be done by making enrollment more liberal and services more long term, by serving all young mothers in the high school, or even by recruiting from other nearby high schools. Program scope depends largely on your definition of the "neediest" portion of the target population, whether you have chosen a site or a site has chosen you, and levels of school and community support.

Laboratory centers offer more extensive programs, designed to provide vocational training for child care professions. These establish selection and enrollment criteria for infants and toddlers, for student parents, and for other students in the high school interested in becoming child care providers. Child care is the unifying activity of such centers but not necessarily the primary function, which is to address a wider range of needs in the community. Your community may be demanding a more large-scale effort and be willing to pay for it.

Limiting direct services and building a referral network simplifies program operations and encourages program participants to deal with real world service providers rather than becoming too dependent on a single program for assistance. It also serves to integrate the program more fully into the community service network, as it encourages interaction and communication. Alternative service suppliers do not view the center as competing for clients. However, when outside services are insufficient or inconveniently located, need demands that the center provide or arrange some supportive services for itself. Educational services are simplest to provide as most can be arranged within the high school. These are decisions that must be made by the planning committee.

Selecting program components

Program components may be divided into core services and support services. Planners must decide which of the services will be provided directly through the center or indirectly through referral. The mix of direct and referral services differs from program to program.

Core services

Infant and toddler care is the primary core service provided by every school-based child care center. Designing a curriculum to meet child care objectives should be a specific priority of the planning effort. Approaches to designing infant/toddler curriculum are discussed in the following chapter.

Educating parents is another core service, although parental education may take a variety of forms, as we have suggested, from teaching basic infant care to comprehensive survival skills. Learning may be structured through individual and group formats and by required enrollment in relevant high school courses. Parents also learn by participating in the operations of the center.

Supportive services

Child care is one part of a wide array of services, which may already be in place in the high school or community or may be developed at a later date. A child care center should be viewed as contributing to the overall network of services.

Supportive services address the wider range of adolescent parents' needs and may be provided by the school, through access to the school nurse, psychologist, social worker, or dietician, or by referral to cooperating community agencies. Referrals are typically handled by the program director or by a school social worker. For convenience, supportive services may be divided into four categories.

Basic necessities: food, clothing, housing. Strategy: providing assistance with AFDC or WIC applications and referral to other community social welfare agencies.

Physical health: preventive well baby care, pre- and post-natal care for the mother, infant development assessment, nutrition, and family planning assistance. Strategy: referral to community health care professionals.

Counseling: counseling for mothers and fathers to aid adjustment to parenting. (Counseling may also be offered for the grandparents—the parents of student parents—to encourage their direct involvement in child care.) Strategy: referral to community mental health facilities, the school psychologist, clergy.

Education: employment, career, and academic counseling, consumer education, family life education. Strategy: integration into established school curricula; referral to high school guidance and vocational counselors.

In the first years of implementation the bulk of start-up funding is typically used to create the necessary physical and developmental environment of the center. Meeting other needs of mothers may be temporarily postponed until the basic infrastructure is in place. Exceptions are laboratory centers with strong educational and vocational components that are administered through the high school and not by the center itself.

Designing curricula

Central to effective program design are the curricula, which should further elaborate program objectives. For example, an objective that focuses on child development should lead to a curriculum that will ensure close monitoring of each infant's health, physical growth, and emotional-social development as measured against established criteria. An objective stressing the acquisition of parenting skills would suggest provision of group activities, counseling, or "rap sessions" built around these issues. Integration of parents in day-to-day center operations would allow hands-on experience under supervision. If one of the program's goals is to improve parents' employability, then ways to incorporate them into established vocational programs should be outlined. Just as objectives are tied to priority of needs, curricula should be a natural outgrowth of program objectives.

Curricula should encompass the envisioned scope of the program. Hand-in-hand with outlined curricula, the planning committee should explore the range of program options that are available with the intent of matching possible components with curricula demands.

The infant/toddler curriculum and curricula for parents are discussed in more detail in the following chapters and should be reviewed before putting together a proposal and requesting funding.

Center and school links

In designing a school-based child care center it is important to consider how the center's operations will be linked to those of the high school and the school system and how the operations will be coordinated. The most basic link to the high school is that the mothers are students in the school. Since a major objective of school-based child care is to help young mothers to remain in and graduate from school, the mothers are usually required to maintain a satisfactory grade average and attend school regularly. None of the centers studied allow children to be left at the center when parents are absent. Making sure that the mothers fulfill these obligations involves working closely with school personnel.

Other program components can provide additional links between center and school. If the center requires the mothers to enroll in child development, parenting, or life skills courses, then these courses need to be developed in coordination with the corresponding school departments. Typical courses and program components are explored in "Programming for Mothers," Chapter 7, and "The Center as a Learning Lab," Chapter 8.

In order to coordinate activities, center planners and staff will have to work with other school personnel on program design and administration. Design is not only a step in establishing a center, but also, in the best of programs, an ongoing process both of evaluation (most often informal) and of improvement. Administration includes scheduling, financial arrangements, and monitoring of the student mothers' status.

How closely the center is linked to the school and to various departments and what types of coordination are necessary depends not only on program activities, but also on the origin of the program, funding arrangements, and administrative oversight. In Detroit, the Murray-Wright Infant–Toddler Child Development Center originated as a child development laboratory in the vocational education department and, consequently, is closely integrated into the departments.

Links may change when funding sources are altered. In general, more sources of outside funding allow the center greater autonomy of operations. The more a program is integrated into a school district's budget, the more it falls under the direct supervision of the school district's central office. There are advantages and disadvantages to both extremes. With outside funding, a program has more autonomy but may tend to remain an add-on, or peripheral, program. Direct funding from the school district endows the program with a more permanent status, allows programs to take advantage of system-provided benefits and services, and prods educators to take the needs of student parents seriously.

In some cases, a center may be attached to but not incorporated into the school and/or school system administration. In Fort Worth, the Polytechnic Child Care Center is not administered by the Fort Worth Independent School System but is subcontracted by the school system to the YWCA. The center is funded primarily by outside funds obtained by the Adolescent Pregnancy Advisory Committee. As a result, the center is operated largely as a separate entity within the school. In this case, most program links, and therefore coordination, are between the center and the YWCA, which provides a number of services to adolescent parents, all of which are supervised by the YWCA's Teen Parent Program Coordinator.

Because of the subcontracting arrangement, the Polytechnic center's bond to the school system is largely through Fort Worth Independent School District's Adolescent Pregnancy Services coordinator, who supervises the center and is very involved in its operations. The only scheduled meeting between center and school staff is when the Adolescent Pregnancy Services coordinator and the center director (who is hired and supervised by the YWCA) meet with the Polytechnic principal before school begins each fall in order to plan the year's activities.

In contrast, the LYFE program at Bay Ridge High School in Brooklyn is funded and administered entirely by the New York City Board of Education, and coordination between the center and the high school is extensive. The head teacher meets at least once a month with the high school principal. Depending on the issues to be discussed, the meeting might also include the social worker or all of the center staff.

The head teacher also meets regularly with the assistant principal of guidance. The center's head teacher is considered to be a part of the high school teaching staff and as such attends the school's teacher meetings, which are twice a month.

Whenever possible, center staff should maintain close contact with high school staff. Integration of center activities and personnel into the world of the high school can only serve to improve the assistance offered to students. Furthermore, if teachers and administrators feel they are a part of the center, they may support it more actively and be able to help identify potential problems, students in need of help, and areas for future expansion.

The principal of the high school must top the list of key personnel with whom to work. A strong relationship with the principal is crucial to both programmatic and administrative coordination. Guidance staff are also very important in helping the mothers cope with their responsibilities.

CHAPTER FIVE

Staff

Staff are the heart and soul of any program. They must be selected carefully and then allowed to shape the programming and to participate in the management process. Their energy, commitment, and skills are the key to the center's success. Therefore it is critical that their well-being become a primary and ongoing priority for planners and administrators.

Qualifications

An individual is chosen to work in child care because of his or her education, experience, and capacity to relate in an effective yet gentle way with parents and children. Infants and toddlers require security, affection, unflagging attention, and a safe environment that encourages learning. To meet these needs, a child care worker has to be hard working, sensitive, emotionally stable, sensible, flexible, patient, imaginative, and respectful of individual differences. He or she must be able to encourage a child's development through play, through appropriate activities, through communication, and through serving as a role model. Working with young children is an extremely demanding role. In addition, the worker must be able to establish a rapport with adolescents and assist them appropriately. Finally, most child care workers agree that no one can survive in a center very long without a sense of humor.

The best centers seem to employ a range of personality types in a complementary blend of intelligence and emotion, introversion and extroversion. Building such a blend is often the result of exercising professional judgment and common sense.

Staff roles

In most centers each child care worker has a formal and specific set of responsibilities and a corresponding job title: director/coordinator, teacher/assistant director, assistant teacher/caregiver, volunteer. The center must also arrange for additional service personnel: physician, nurse, social worker, counselor, and kitchen, maintenance, and office staff. Some of the staff will be full-time, others part-time or contracted on a consultant basis, such as health personnel and counselors.

The director, teachers, and assistants are typically paid by the center, while others may donate their time or be paid by a sponsoring agency as an in-kind service. Staffing a center requires an understanding of how each of these positions interacts and contributes to the good of the whole. Every worker is in a position to make a unique contribution to the program.

Staffing strategies

The number and complexity of tasks, and decisions about who is responsible for these tasks, depend on the program's size and scope, its structure and relationship with sponsoring agencies, and the breakdown of budgeting between administrative and child care duties.

Adult-child ratios

All centers need staff who work directly with the children and are responsible for planning and implementing the program on a daily basis. The number of these staff members is usually established by law as a set ratio of adults to infants and to toddlers: for example, one adult to five infants and one adult to six toddlers, as in Texas. Licensing requirements may also be more specific. In Tennessee, staffing ratios are broken down by ages:

Age	Ratio
1–15 months	1:5
15–35 months	1:8
combined ages	1:6
3 years old	1:10

These ratios may be met with various mixes of teachers, assistants, and volunteers but never with *all* assistants or *all* volunteers. Qualified full-time teachers must bear full responsibility for the children in their care and be present to provide direction for other workers. In smaller centers, the director often doubles as a teacher and takes shifts with the children in between his or her administrative tasks. In larger centers, child care and administrative duties tend to be more segregated. Administrative personnel spend most of their time in an office, handling liaison with the school and other agencies and taking care of bookkeeping, while teachers stay "on the floor." In the director's absence, one individual, sometimes titled the head teacher, should be in charge of staff and activities and should be present at all times.

Staff assignments

The ages and abilities of children in the program influence grouping and child/staff assignments. Many experts recommend that teachers should be in charge of a mix of ages and developmental stages so that no one staff member is responsible for all crib infants, all climbers and walkers, or all of the easier, or more difficult, babies. For example, if three- to eighteen-month-old children are grouped together, then infants can be assigned in pairs to the staff and toddlers similarly grouped. Too many fussy babies are as difficult to handle for a single adult as too many active climbers and walkers. Initially, one adult is assigned to aid a new infant's adjustment to the center environment. However, as they pass into new stages of development, all children are generally expected to circulate to all staff members. Such groupings shift in response to the needs of children and parents, and to the needs and preferences of the staff members themselves.

Staggered shifts and job combining

Programs that we visited used two major staffing strategies: staggered shifts and job combining. With staggered shifts, as many staff as possible work in overlapping shifts. Full-time personnel, depending on the center's hours, may work nine hours one day, from opening to closing, and seven hours the next, coming in later or leaving early. Part-time persons or volunteers are brought in for the peak hours in the morning and afternoon and to cover weekly staff meetings or planning sessions. Each employee specializes in specific duties.

Job combining is a more collective approach. Child care and many administrative tasks are divided among all full- and part-time staff members. The director doubles as a teacher and teacher substitute. Teachers handle some administrative or public relations duties. Assistants may have child care responsibilities and be called on to prepare snacks. Tasks are clearly understood, yet individual roles are less defined. Such an arrangement usually requires a weekly staff meeting in which responsibilities are defined and the week's duties assigned.

Staggered shifts seem to predominate in larger centers, while job combining occurs more frequently in smaller centers with limited staff. The first approach is more precise and patterned, the second more flexible.

Full-time and part-time employees

Full-time employees provide continuity. A few centers have tried hiring exclusively part-time personnel to save on payroll costs by not offering vacation, sick leave, health insurance, and other costs associated with full-time staff. But these savings resulted in high turnover, low commitment, and low morale with a negative impact on the overall quality of the program. While part-time positions are an essential adjunct to full-time positions, they cannot carry the program on their own. Teacher assistants are often hired on a part-time basis at the employees' own request. These employees may have other full-time jobs or home responsibilities and desire the additional income or a chance to work with children. Teachers, however, should be full-time employees to meet the children's need for stable, long-term relationships.

Volunteers

All of the centers visited used volunteers in some capacity. In a large center, administrative tasks can easily fill the director's day, limiting time for interaction with staff and children. Often, administrative duties, such as accounting and payroll, can be subcontracted or handled by volunteers. Senior citizen volunteers were a resource to many of the centers visited. Besides assisting in child care they contributed office work, answered inquiries, or handled public relations for the center. Their presence and experience can make a valuable contribution to the center's atmosphere.

Volunteers can also help teachers by assisting with routine child care tasks. All volunteer/child interactions, however, should be closely supervised by teachers. In no centers were volunteers allowed to supervise children on their own or work with children if they were not suitable.

Volunteers can be recruited from community service organizations, such as senior citizen groups or local college organizations. Not only child study departments, but also student volunteer and social organizations, such as fraternities and sororities, are excellent sources for volunteers. The Junior League in many cities provides volunteer mentors for programs serving young mothers. Many organizations encourage their members to volunteer in the public service, and child care is one of the most attractive forms of volunteering.

Although volunteers can provide invaluable assistance to a child care center by giving extra attention to children and by being an "extra pair of hands" for teachers, they are not always dependable, particularly those accepted with no references. Often, volunteers will feel that, because they are donating their time, they can show up or not show, as they please. Centers that depend on volunteers to round out their staff require more consistency.

For this reason, centers use volunteers almost solely from structured volunteer programs. Structured programs schedule volunteers (thus saving center administrators time and headaches), monitor their behavior, and are sensitive to the director's suggestions or complaints. In addition, structured programs often provide participants with special training or counseling to aid their work. While exceptions should always be made for outstanding individuals, planners should not attempt to handle the difficulties of scheduling individual volunteers on an ongoing basis.

Today's volunteer, through commitment, ability, and longevity, can easily become tomorrow's employee. Therefore, a well-structured volunteer program can provide the center with a labor pool of experienced and proven workers.

Students and student parents

Laboratory centers are in a special position to use students on a regularly scheduled basis. Students may voluntarily participate in the center, as part of home economics, family education, child care, or other relevant course work. They may also become involved through work-study or other school-sponsored vocational programs.

Centers that encourage participation of mothers schedule time in the center for mothers to help with care, feeding, and clean-up, usually immediately before and after school hours and especially during lunch. Some centers make parental participation of five to ten hours per week a requisite of program enrollment. Play sessions are sometimes arranged during student off-times, such as study halls, although care must be taken to avoid interfering with other course work. Center staff, working closely with the high school office, can establish a policy that considers the student's performance and capabilities.

At all times staff must strive to understand the young parent's perspective. Strong feelings of protectiveness, of guilt, fear, and worry may influence a mother's response to staff activities. The rationale for all activities and decisions should be carefully explained, and a mother's observations and opinions respected.

Authority for defining roles and responsibilities

Depending on administrative structures and funding arrangements, school district administrators may be responsible for deciding job descriptions, qualifications, and hiring procedures. Often, funding is channeled through the school board, which accepts responsibility for overseeing center operations. The school system may be responsible for paying the director and teachers. If the center is on school grounds, it is under the jurisdiction of the principal and must comply with school policies. In such cases, hiring is normally done through the personnel office. Job descriptions and qualifications will already be an established part of school personnel policies. However, criteria used by personnel offices are not always designed to select specialized child care workers and should be fine-tuned for the center. The most commonly added criteria are that the director and teachers have a strong academic background and experience in child development. The advisory board may ask to assist the school board and personnel office in recruiting and hiring appropriate staff.

A school-based center incorporates additional program components beyond daily child care, such as parenting education, vocational education, and referrals, which require strong interpersonal and teaching skills. These additional program demands will also influence roles, responsibilities, and therefore hiring criteria.

Job descriptions

Whether the center's board is independent or subject to school administrators, it will probably want to develop its own set of job descriptions. Most child care center planners developed formal job descriptions for all key staff positions to serve as hiring guidelines, as a measure of expectations for working staff, and as criteria for formal evaluation of the employee's performance. A job description should include a definition of role and responsibilities and a description of the position (full- or part-time, temporary or permanent).

Planners can use a few basic questions as a starting point for designing staff positions:
- What will the role of the staff member be in the center's daily operations?
- What will his or her position be in the authority structure?
- What will the responsibilities of the staff member be? Which responsibilities are dictated by state and local regulations?
- What qualifications must the individual have?
- Will the position be full- or part-time?
- Who will pay the staff member?

The director

The director is the key position of any center. Above all, he or she must be a wise educator and a capable leader. The director must coordinate activities within the center and serve as liaison with the advisory board, the school board, school district administrators, the high school principal, referral agencies, parents, and the general public—a demanding role. The director must support the rationale underlying all aspects of the program. Organizational skills are essential, and public relations skills indispensable. Directors are diplomats; they must be effective communicators. The ability to structure ideas and express them clearly provides the foundation for leadership within the center and for liaison without. Personal skills as well as education and experience should be considered when setting eligibility requirements.

The director is solely and directly responsible to the governing body of the center. He or she must conduct the program in accordance with policies established by the governing body, inform the governing body of progress and inadequacies within the program, and aid the governing body in formulating new and revising old policies by adequately representing the recommendations of staff.

Certain administrative tasks must be accomplished daily, others periodically. The director must oversee administrative tasks even if they are managed by someone else. These nonteaching tasks include:

- implementing and refining program curricula;
- supervising and training program personnel;
- conducting regular staff meetings;
- overseeing enrollment procedures;
- orienting new mothers;
- hiring and orienting new staff;
- maintaining records and monitoring the budget;
- doing the payroll and ordering supplies;
- writing proposals and communicating with funding sources; and
- maintaining good public relations.

The program director is responsible for managing money and materials, but more importantly, he or she is responsible for managing people. Staff that are effectively and sensitively led will make the difference between a mediocre program, which nevertheless runs in the black, and an excellent program that is innovative and can change lives. An effective director is a teacher of teachers.

Teachers become the director's sounding board for new ideas; their opinions need to be solicited and respected. Individual accomplishments should be publicly acknowledged. Teachers should be encouraged to try new solutions and given the latitude to fail and the guidance to learn from their mistakes. A good director will challenge the teacher to excel by working on problems and solutions. If the program design is sufficiently challenging and if teachers are entrusted with shaping important pieces of it, then most will rise to their responsibility. Such leadership results in a dynamic child care operation that benefits children, young mothers, and staff.

The governing body may desire a particular expertise to fulfill the program design, or licensing regulations may specify further requirements, but the following can serve as a general guideline for determining the director's qualifications. An administrative director should have:

- a graduate degree plus two years experience in administering or supervising a similar program; or
- a bachelor of arts or bachelor of science degree plus four years of relevant work experience, including administration and supervision.

To serve as an educational director, the candidate should have:

- a college degree with course emphasis in early childhood education; plus
- a minimum of two years experience as a group teacher of children under the age of six; plus
- one year's experience supervising an educational program.

A position that combines both administrative and educational roles will require some combination of qualifications from both categories. Any experience working with pregnant and parenting adolescents and disadvantaged students should be considered a large plus.

The director can be recruited from the ranks of the community support network. In several cases, the center's first director was chosen from among those individuals who were involved in the planning process from the beginning. Lyn Overholt of the Preschool/Parenting Learning Center and Carol Burt-Beck of the Bay Ridge LYFE Program originated their programs and were selected to implement them by virtue of their education, experience, and demonstrated commitment. Both were selected and hired through the school board. In these instances, the individuals had demonstrated their ability to organize, support, and design a workable program; for the school board to bring in someone from the outside to implement the program would have been unthinkable.

The director for the Fort Worth program, on the other hand, was chosen by the Board of Directors of the YWCA, the subcontracting agency. The board established a search committee to seek out a local resident with the following qualifications: teaching experience, experience with developmentally delayed children, an interest and expertise in the area of adolescent pregnancy, and proven administrative skills. Word circulated through the adolescent pregnancy network, and nominations were accepted from board members, the school board, and other participating agencies.

The director and two coordinators for the Infant–Toddler Center at Murray-Wright High School, Detroit, were recruited by word of mouth and hired through the school personnel office, with recommendations from the high school principal and the center's advisory board. Applications were preferred from home economics teachers with education and experience in child development. A committee interviewed candidates and made recommendations to the personnel office for the final selection. The process was supervised by school administration and the Vocational Education Department.

Teachers and teacher assistants

Teachers are directly responsible to the director for their work. A teacher's responsibilities within the center will include but not be limited to:
- monitoring the health, safety, and well-being of all children in their charge;
- directing the activities of assistants;
- planning and supervising children's daily activities;
- preparing necessary educational materials;
- keeping classrooms in order and equipment in good condition;
- maintaining case files for each child;
- sharing information and observations with all staff members; and
- communicating with parents about their child's development and daily activities.

The educational and experiential qualifications for meeting these responsibilities may include:
- a bachelor of arts degree in education with student teaching experience at the early childhood level; or
- an associate in arts, associate in science, or associate in applied science degree plus two years' experience in a supervised child care or Head Start program; or
- two years of college work, plus one or two years of experience in an assistant teacher role in a supervised educational program.

Educational requirements for teachers vary significantly from center to center, depending on the demands of the curricula and licensing requirements. Teachers must be state certified and have a current teaching license. This usually requires a certificate in early childhood development. School-based centers, especially, need to be concerned with finding teachers who can implement the educational components of the program with a minimum of training and supervision.

To a young child, the assistant teacher, teacher aide, or child care giver can be as important as the teacher. The child's personality or needs may allow him or her to relate more closely to one adult or another, regardless of their relative status within the program. At times, circumstances will require that the assistant teacher take over for the teacher, and he or she must be prepared and qualified to do so. Depending on state licensing requirements, an assistant teacher may need only a high school diploma, while, in other states, he or she may need virtually the same qualifications as the teacher.

If allowed the choice, many center directors seem to prefer experience and personal qualifications over schooling and are willing to waive some educational requirements, if an individual seems otherwise capable.

Teachers and teacher assistants are recruited through advertising in local newspapers and by notices posted in schools and service agencies. Respondents are then screened according to established criteria, which specify the education and experience required. Advertisements normally give a salary range to prescreen applicants. Salaries may then be adjusted to the high or low end of this range, according to the applicant's qualifications.

Service personnel

Service personnel, such as janitors, cooks, and accountants, are often supplied by the school system or other sponsoring agency as an in-kind service to the center. If they are to be hired directly by the center, then advertising is the accepted method of recruitment.

Hiring practices

Hiring practices vary. The school system may be responsible for hiring the director or all personnel through the personnel office. The center's board may hire the director of the program, who is then responsible for hiring all other staff, according to established criteria. In some centers, the board takes a more active role in interviewing applicants or approving the director's selections. These oversight activities provide checks on the director's authority and may be necessary with specific governance or funding arrangements. Circumstances and preference will dictate which system is adopted.

Procedure

Hiring proceeds in several steps. The center accepts written applications for employment or résumés submitted in response to its ads. All applications should be sorted according to qualifications and kept on file. An individual may be recalled at a later date for a new opening or different position. Prospective employees are then called in for an interview to determine their suitability for the position. Interviews tend to be informal and may include a tour of the facilities and a description of the program's objectives and operations. By sharing information about the center, try to encourage the applicant to express his or her own goals, experiences, and opinions.

Interviewers should prepare a checklist of the personal qualities they are seeking. If the director is solely responsible for hiring, another staff member should be present during the interview to provide a second opinion. References should be required and thoroughly checked. Some states require that child care workers be checked for a criminal record as some offenses preclude working with children. Even if it is not required, it is a good idea. If qualifications, personality, and references all check out, then a decision is made to hire the applicant. Often, two applicants may seem equally qualified for a position and need to be recalled for a second interview before a decision can be made. This same procedure is followed by the board when hiring the director.

Salaries

Salaries will be based on the going rate for similar work in the community and for similar skills and experience comparable to those required by the program. The board may wish to set the base pay, or starting rate, at a moderate level and build in incentive raises up to a maximum rate. If the labor market is tight, the wage and salary structure might have to be increased to attract properly qualified personnel. This is a matter of fine-tuning as funding sources may prove hesitant to allocate money for salaries that seem too high.

Salaries in child care centers are almost always low. As most staff are women, and frequently important breadwinners in their families, the wages offered to child care workers contribute to the inferior economic position of women workers. In addition, low pay inevitably translates into rapid staff turn over. Therefore it is important for planners and administrators to negotiate the best wages and benefits possible for their staff. In addition, incentive raises can be used to reward the best workers and keep them with the program. Workers with more skills and experience and those who put forth extra effort should be better paid.

Personnel files

Employee files include the résumé and application for employment, notes from employment interviews, home and emergency telephone numbers, information on salary and benefits, medical records, record of any problems with the work of the employee, and copies of performance evaluations.

Formal performance evaluations, done on a periodic basis by the employee's supervisor, are considered by some to be a useful tool for reviewing mutual expectations, deciding on salary raises and promotions, and determining training interests and needs. Evaluations are sometimes done by establishing a scale for various categories, such as dependability, role effectiveness, attitude, initiative, and overall performance. Scores for each category can be added together to identify an individual performance rating. Often program administrators hold regular supervisory conferences with each staff member in order to discuss and review working relationships as well as job performance.

A supportive work environment

Child care tends to attract highly motivated and committed individuals who are often willing to sacrifice in pay what they gain in job satisfaction. Child care centers benefit from this commitment, and planners should encourage but take care not to exploit it.

The centers visited by our observers did their best to provide a comfortable and supportive work environment. Much of this depended on the director, who was called upon to set the right tone for the center. This quality results from a mix of effective communications, concern, responsiveness, democratic decision making, and other variables, which are not easy to pin down. A heavy-handed authority, wielded with little concern for staff suggestions, opinions, or emotions, quickly leads to conflict, resistance, and a high staff turnover. Staff members who feel unappreciated or used are likely to transfer these emotions to the children, sabotaging the harmony of the center. They are likely to quit over a problem rather than try to solve it. Tone is an intangible element, but experienced child care staff agree that it derives from the top down. Administrators' and directors' behaviors and attitudes toward staff members will be replicated throughout the center, both good and bad.

Centers also take care to maintain proper staffing levels to prevent overworking a few dedicated individuals. Overwork leads all too quickly to the common condition known as staff burnout, which manifests in lethargy, inattention, short temper, even illness. Everyone has a breaking point, whether or not they want to acknowledge it. The director should be aware when others are worked too hard and act to ease the situation. But the director is also susceptible and needs to monitor his or her own behavior. Snapping at an employee over some small or imagined mistake is a sure symptom that burnout is approaching, and the whole center will suffer as a result of a dedication that doesn't know when to rest. Child care is a mentally and emotionally demanding occupation with its own set of occupational hazards.

Another consideration for a supportive work environment is to allow space—both physical and mental—for the staff to be alone during the working day. All staff members should have a place to retreat, and specific times should be set aside during the day for breaks. This allows the staff member to jot down observations, plan the next segment's activities, and generally unwind. Periods of introverted activity decrease anxiety and increase the staff member's effectiveness. Small considerations such as these will pay large dividends in terms of employee satisfaction.

Individuals who choose to work as caregivers of children are usually aware of the budget constraints of most centers, but they desire the fulfillment of working closely with children. While there can be no substitute for paying a reasonable wage, the center can work to enhance those aspects of the job that most reward the employee, and it can express appreciation for a job well done.

Staff development

Because of the children's rapid growth and developmental change, caregivers must be particularly flexible in their actions and able to adapt promptly to changing needs. Therefore, in-service training is an essential component of any program. The director or head teacher should encourage staff to develop observational skills by informally sharing his or her knowledge of developmental stages and by drawing the staff's attention to them as they occur. The ability to observe children objectively and to understand observations in terms of growth and development are essential skills for competent caregivers. These skills enable staff to learn more from what they are seeing every day. Because similar behaviors take on different meanings as a child develops, staff should be taught to view behaviors from the child's perspective and to understand it intuitively.

Weekly staff meetings, as well as special workshops on particular topics, are used in most centers. In Brooklyn, the LYFE center schedules weekly staff meetings and periodic workshops on relevant topics. Calley Bittel, the head teacher, has found it constructive to ask the staff to suggest topics they want to address. Topics have included: music activities, conflicting expectations of behavior (thumbsucking), and discipline issues (biting). She finds that workshops allowing hands-on learning are most effective.

At the center in Elizabeth, New Jersey, the head teacher meets weekly with each child care worker to discuss their problems and observations and to determine how each child in their charge is developing, according to the individualized teaching plan. These meetings are viewed as an opportunity to provide direction for teachers, to encourage them to articulate their observations, and to participate in planning.

Staff training and development are essential center activities. Both time and money should be budgeted for meetings and training sessions. Periodically, the center may wish to bring in specialists, such as university professors, high school department heads, or other child care center directors, to discuss topics in child care and development. In addition, the director should introduce such educational materials and teaching aids as seem appropriate.

In working with student parents, staff will want to focus some of their training time on topics related to teenage pregnancy, adolescence, the position of women in American society, the problems facing youngsters with low basic academic skills, and the like. The aim of this training should be to strengthen the capacity for empathy among staff as well as to increase knowledge.

CHAPTER SIX

Infant/Toddler Program

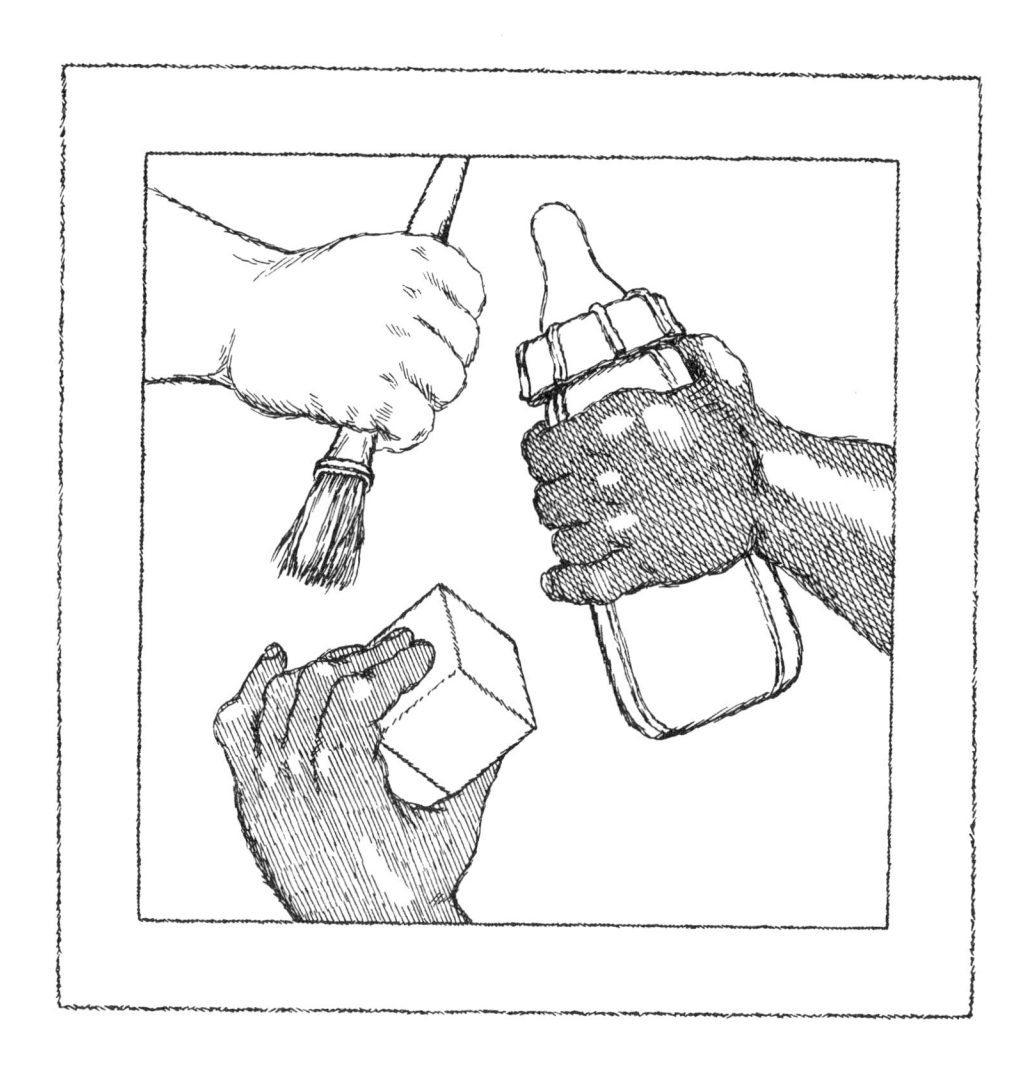

Care for young children is neither a scaled-down version of care for older children nor merely babysitting. Infant/toddler care is determined by the unique characteristics of infants and toddlers, whose first three years of life include rapid physical, social, emotional, and cognitive development. Furthermore, as the infant or toddler is more dependent on the caregiver and therefore more vulnerable to adversity, a child care center must be organized to protect, nurture, and encourage children.

A sound child care program for babies and small children must offer a safe environment, a stimulating yet developmentally appropriate structure and activities, and relationships with staff that ensure emotional security. Only in a milieu that is *safe, stimulating, and secure* will all children prosper and grow.

A good learning environment for young children is one that supports their innate interest in the world around them. Children are learning constantly. At first, and for a long time, they gather information through their senses. Later, language becomes a usable tool for collecting information. As children collect information, they order and reorder it, forming concepts of themselves, their caregivers, and their world. Their learning is enhanced by adults who highlight and enrich their daily experiences through offering a carefully designed sequence of developmentally appropriate experiences and through communicating with children about the center's routines and their responses to it.

The structure and events of the children's day at your center provide a rich array of opportunities for learning. Take snacktime, for example: Sitting down at a table with other children is a new experience for a twelve-month-old child entering a child care program. Over time, the child "collects" basic information about snacktime. As this child becomes older, he or she eventually begins to anticipate and describe, for example, juice and will be eager to assist with snack preparation and serving. The caregiver's skill and care with program design and language help youngsters develop a basic vocabulary and organize concepts.

Talking about the child's experiences in age-appropriate language is especially important. By discussing a child's actions, a teacher encourages the child to talk and conceptualize. By helping a child develop words for feelings, a caregiver enables the child to develop positive ways for coping with sadness, anger, frustration, jealousy, and all the other feeling states children experience.

The center's approach to children benefits their parents as well. Teachers model roles for parents by telling them about their child's activities, reactions, and mastery of new skills. Caregivers show parents how subtle, incremental developments are important to the staff, to the parent, and to the child.

In creating a program for children and adolescent parents, your approach will be enhanced by knowing the developmental sequences for infant and child development. This will allow you to plan for the phase-specific needs of the growing child.

Theories of child development and applications

We now have a large body of sophisticated information about early human development. The research and theories of Erik Erikson, Jean Piaget, Anna Freud, and Mahler/Pine/Bergman predominate and are reflected in the many fine guides written for parents and teachers. You will want to be sure your center has a program that is grounded in our best understanding of what young children need.

The distinct needs of very young children can be conceptualized in terms of three different age levels: Infant (0–9 months), Mobile Infant (6–19 months), and Toddler (16–36 months). The needs of infants, mobile infants, and toddlers overlap because children develop at different rates. Staff and parents should expect each child to be unique and to develop on his/her own timetable. Average child development includes both growth and regression. Regression often occurs after a child's illness, after a vacation from the center, and with the birth of siblings.

From birth to three years old, the child moves from being totally dependent on caregivers to becoming increasingly independent, capable of sustaining attachments to other humans, of physical control and dexterity, and of communicating with language. Dr. Margaret S. Mahler describes these first stages of human development as the separation/individuation process, during which the child gradually gains a sense of self as separate from the mother.

Erik Erikson describes a developing child's tasks as learning trust and learning autonomy. Basic trust, instilled by quality relationships, gives the child a sense of being "all right" in the world. Learning autonomy comes by making choices within safe, clearly defined limits.

Certain patterns of relationships and space design are optimal for supporting children's development. The staff-to-child ratio needs to be low enough to allow for a consistent relationship between each child and one or two special caregivers. This allows a feeling of closeness, of attachment, and of trust to develop between infant and caregiver. The physical space must be regular, dependable, and comfortable to convey a feeling of consistency as well.

Jean Piaget describes how repeated manipulation of objects, such as toys—he calls this functional play—allows the child to see the outcome of action and interaction. From having no cognitive structures at birth, merely reflex structures, the child develops:

- the ability to classify and relate objects at four to eight months;
- the ability to engage in primitive means-end behavior at eight to twelve months;
- the facility to solve problems by the age of eighteen to thirty-six months; and
- the capacity for representational thought (at nine to twenty-four months) so that he or she can represent stimuli from the inside and the outside, and therefore organize his or her inner world.

Staff can facilitate this process by allowing children to experiment with new materials appropriate for their level of development either on their own or with adults. Caregivers must be willing to permit risk taking and decision making. They are responsible for ensuring that the child can take appropriate risks without danger.

Children in child care are separated from their mothers for many hours during the day. They respond to this separation differently. From birth until four to eight months, because they are less able to differentiate among individuals, babies are primarily interested in their own comfort and less concerned about who provides it. Between four and six months, the baby shows unmistakable signs that he or she recognizes his/her parents. Thereafter babies are likely to have adverse reactions to people who are not mother. This is often called stranger anxiety. This developmental milestone indicates that the child has learned to differentiate "mother" from "other." The child is beginning to develop a sense of his or her own separateness.

While children's negative reactions to separation are absolutely normal, they pose a challenge for your center. Many of your children will have difficulty being left by the mother or responding to her when she returns. To help children cope with separation during these phases, center planners should:

- structure the program so that each child can develop a special and consistent relationship with one or two caregivers who will be the substitute "home base" for the child in the mother's absence;
- allow children to develop their separation rituals;
- plan center routines as a source of reassurance (transitions should be cued by repeated events, such as playing the same prelunch record each day);
- encourage parents to develop departure rituals at home (the baby can "help" get a coat, close the door, turn off the light) as preparation for coming to the center;
- allow each child to have special objects in the center that are reminders of home, such as a special blanket, or a rattle, or a cap. These "transitional objects" should be kept in a specific place where the child can reach them;
- design games that encourage infants to learn the logic of the world and not fear that people will disappear on them (the classic peek-a-boo serves this purpose in an enjoyable way). Staff and parents can incorporate other activities in which objects/people disappear and return; and
- use specific props to help children cope with the mother's absence, such as pictures of the children's families that can be used by staff to structure conversations with the children.

Some developmental characteristics and appropriate playthings to make

BIRTH TO THREE MONTHS

Developmental characteristics

looking

tracking moving objects

responds to sound by looking in direction of sound

can hold small rattle briefly if placed in hand

smiles in response to a person

finds hands

Appropriate playthings

mobile

rattle

soft "doughnut" of cloth

large crib pictures of faces or very bold, simple patterns like checkerboard

soft doll or animal

THREE TO SIX MONTHS

Developmental characteristics

holds head upright and rotates it from side to side

smiles and laughs

plays with hands and feet

babbles

rolls over

reaches for, grasps and mouths objects

enjoys bath

distinguishes "mother" from others

Appropriate playthings

floating bath toys

rattles: use covered juice cans, film canisters, filled with sound-making objects

mobile with activator: baby pulls string and mobile moves

crib mirror

objects of various shapes for manipulating

SIX TO NINE MONTHS

Developmental characteristics

can see effects of own actions

sits alone

crawls

pulls self to standing position

uses both hands to manipulate objects, hits one object against another, transfers toy from one hand to another

looks for toy that disappears

uncovers toy hidden by cloth

explores toy with eyes and fingers

imitates sounds, vocalizes

may react with anxiety to strangers

enjoys rhythm, music, singing

responds to name, understands some requests

begins to differentiate self

Appropriate playthings

"busy board" with objects to manipulate

drop-in toys

hiding bags and objects

"drum"—coffee can and spoon

rolling toys—oatmeal containers with string, filled with jar tops

textured wall hanging with bright colors

box filled with a variety of textured and interestingly shaped objects

Source: Dr. Nancy Balaban, Director, Infant and Parent Development Program, Bank Street College of Education, New York, NY

NINE TO TWELVE MONTHS

Developmental characteristics

anticipates events (mother's coat signals leaving)

intentional behavior begins (drops and throws objects, pushes food away)

active search behavior for hidden objects

repeats own actions

first words

responds to heights and size

uses thumb and forefinger to pick up

crawls

beginning to walk or walk with support

likes to carry things

shows toy preferences

enjoys pat-a-cake, peek-a-boo, bye-bye

puts on object inside another

Appropriate playthings

nesting and stacking cans

drop-in and come-out toys made of bleach bottles or oatmeal containers

egg carton as a base for holding cardboard tubes

juice can "telescope" to look through

books on heavy cardboard with large pictures of everyday objects

mirror

pots, pans, coffeepots

TWELVE TO EIGHTEEN MONTHS

Developmental characteristics

walking becomes secure

locomotion is paramount (climbing, sliding, jumping, etc.)

language is developing and important

may display intense separation feelings

"no" is a favorite word

has "a love affair with the world" (Greenacre)

feeds self

finds hidden objects

goes off on his own and comes back for "emotional refueling"

repeats own actions as he "practices" skills

follows simple commands

enjoys pictures

gathering and dumping activities, peek-a-boo are prime activities

Appropriate playthings

ball—to roll, hide, throw, chase, etc.

totes—buckets, plus "things" to collect and dump

books

simple puzzles

instruments: drum, shakers, etc.

blocks (milk cartons)

boxes for sitting on, crawling into, climbing on, etc.

pull and push toys

dolls and animals

pots, pans, etc.

EIGHTEEN TO TWENTY-FOUR MONTHS

Developmental characteristics

climbs, jumps, runs well

begins fantasy play, "feeds" doll, etc.

combines words, uses simple sentences

obstinate behavior often seen

eager to "show" adult his discoveries

helps dress and undress self

imitates adult actions

in motion

idea of self becoming more clear

anxious about separation from mothering person

toilet training begun

Appropriate playthings

two- or three-piece puzzles made from magazine pictures

carton filled with cornmeal, rice, etc.

play cube: cut opening in large carton for crawling in and out

touching book: with different kinds of textures

doll cradle made from mushroom or tomato basket

pull boxes with strings

totes: use bleach bottles

photo of toddler and parent(s) covered with clear contact, prominently displayed

TWENTY-FOUR TO THIRTY-SIX MONTHS

Developmental characteristics

engages in symbolic play

likes motion and things in motion

interest in peers

speech develops rapidly

repeats and imitates actions of adults and children

"mine" is a favorite word; so is "no"

knows that objects have a permanence and are separate from himself

experiences strong emotions as he moves toward autonomy

experiments with materials and with own abilities

more control over motoric coordination and over toilet functions

often ritualistic

enjoys stories, music, dancing, water play, paints, dough, dress-up

Appropriate playthings

spools (or other objects) for stringing

objects for matching and sorting

musical instruments (shakers, drums, etc.)

sand

water: plastic bottles with and without holes in the bottom; sponges, etc.

buckets for filling and dumping, pulling and pushing

"props" for make-believe; hats, pocketbooks, etc.

books, paints, clay, puzzles, crayons

clothespins and cans: match the colors

cardboard cartons

kitchen objects

Priorities for a quality infant/toddler environment

Staff

The key to a good program lies in the abilities of the staff. An infant care center is people. It is a place where adults set up an environment for very young humans to grow and develop. People are the most important part of the world for children.

Program philosophy

The way in which the program is structured expresses certain values—the importance of the individual as well as the group, of an infant's attachment to one or two consistent caregivers, of limit-setting without abuse, of respect for the parent's culture, of cooperation, of the value of imagination, and so on. The program's underlying beliefs and values should be articulated and shared with parents and other school personnel. This increases understanding of your program, which is important for keeping support from educators and parents.

A safe and healthy environment

A clean facility possessing adequate heat, humidity, lighting, and ventilation (all at floor level where babies are) should be provided. A safe environment requires careful screening of materials and furnishings. And staff must be trained in safe procedures with regard to foods; children who act out negative feelings by hitting, biting, and such; cleanliness routines for personnel and children; arrangement of the space and materials; first aid techniques, and so on.

Personalized care

It is not enough for a baby to be simply kept dry and involved in activities. Each baby needs to feel loved and prized for his/her unique qualities. Care must accommodate the particular needs of each baby, rather than requiring the baby to continually accommodate adult or group schedules and demands. This allows the baby to develop a strong sense of self, a sense of power and individual importance. Thus the environment should be planned to allow for individual differences in sleeping, eating, and toileting schedules.

Organization

Organization is crucial for the children's and staff's well-being. Practical problems—lunch isn't ready, diapers can't be found, a child's "transitional" object is lost—may be extremely disruptive. A policy of "a place for everything and everything in its place" ensures that materials are always accessible when they are needed and allows the staff to remain attentive to the children's needs and not have to be preoccupied with finding missing items.

Appropriate stimulation

Infants can get too much as well as too little stimulation. Providing appropriate stimulation must take into account the number of babies, the size of the space, and the number of caregivers.

Designing the daily program

Your program will be the result of careful arrangement of time, materials, and objectives. This requires blending a program's philosophy of child care and its goals with an understanding of child growth and development to create an approach that the center's staff will follow. Activities, daily routines, and educational materials must be right for your specific group of children. Flexible application of all programming is essential.

The director or a head teacher is responsible for directing the program. In most centers, the director or head teacher consulted with other child development specialists. In several cases, a child development specialist was hired on a part-time basis to assist teachers in setting up the program.

Formal program goals are often informally pursued. For example, one program's goal was to incorporate infant development and stimulation techniques by concentrating on acquisition of language skills, fine and gross motor skills, and personal/social growth. Actual implementation in these areas, however, was left to the discretion of teachers. Teachers were selected for a strong background in child development and allowed to improvise within an informal framework. The formal program consisted of little more than a daily schedule:

- morning sign-in and health check,
- breakfast,
- clean-up and structured activity period,
- naps,
- lunch,
- structured outdoor activities,
- snacks, and
- preparation for leaving and sign-out.

However, a more formal approach has advantages, too. Learning activities are set within a solid theoretical framework and are pursued on an individual or group basis. For example, all of the center's one-year-olds should be given opportunities to play with blocks, but a child who lags behind her peers in small motor coordination might be given additional assistance in manipulating the blocks.

With a standardized learning plan, each child passes through specific learning "gates" that can be recorded, charted, and compared with developmental norms. This information can be used to assess a child's development and for program evaluation purposes. The structure of a more formal program also lends itself to parent education and is helpful when providing vocational training.

In one center, an Individual Educational Profile was kept for each infant and toddler to monitor progress in seven specific areas:

- self-help;
- gross motor skills;
- fine motor skills;
- sensory response;
- language acquisition;
- cognitive development; and
- social-emotional interaction.

Profiles are updated biweekly by the teachers and used as a way of evaluating strengths and weaknesses in teaching techniques and materials.

Specific program requirements for infants and for toddlers are spelled out in some community and state licensing requirements, which should be consulted. These requirements can serve as an outline for any further items that you feel should be included.

What follows are suggestions for organizing activities with specific educational objectives. These should be used in consultation with a child development specialist.

Scheduling

A plan for the day is developed by the teachers for themselves and their children. A schedule must differ for children of different ages. A younger child's attention span and ability to engage in means–end oriented actions is measured in seconds, not minutes. Young children like many short actions. They also need time to rest and pursue more individual interests.

The day should include opportunities for many kinds of activities: one-to-one interaction, group activities, and "free time" when children can choose their play, rest or sleep, meals, special events. One-to-one interaction with a consistent caregiver is very important for building trust between the child and adults and for developing individual skills. Activities in groups—singing, water and sand play, outdoor play, art projects, dance/movement time, listening to a book read aloud—allow children to learn social skills. Group experiences foster cooperation and encourage children to learn about one another in a nonthreatening context.

Individualized programming

The individualized approach uses standardized assessments, a weekly plan, and teacher observations to guide the learning of each child. It is implemented by the director and teachers according to the following steps:

- The individual child is screened, using observations and standardized assessment scales, to determine the relative level of development.
- Long-range skills-acquisition objectives are developed to meet deficiencies determined through screening.
- The teachers determine which skills need to be learned and how to help the child acquire them. Teachers also determine which program materials and equipment will be useful in this process.
- The teachers develop a plan to work with the child on specific skills, using modeling, cuing, encouragement, and praise.
- Instruments are used to evaluate the child's progress toward meeting the objectives of the teaching plan.
- The child's progress is documented through observations and testing.
- The teachers revise and update the teaching plan or teaching method, according to the child's progress.

Screening: The use of assessment scales

Diagnostic tests, based on scales of development, are used in some infant/toddler programs. These assessment scales are used to keep track of individual development and to introduce specific exercises and activities that are matched with a child's level of functioning. Teachers in several centers test all of the children periodically and then structure activities and staff interactions for each child based on the findings.

Formal assessment scales are sometimes used, as described above, to determine what a child is capable of doing. The teacher then translates these capabilities into activities to enhance the individual child's performance. With each new development, new activities are introduced to solidify the child's accomplishments. Centers agree that planning must be individualized, because, although all children go through the same stages, they do not all go at the same pace.

The Bay Ridge LYFE Program's head teacher, Calley Bittel, creates an individualized plan for each child—implemented by that child's assigned caregiver. Using the Early Learning Assessment Profile (ELAP), which is administered every four to six weeks, she draws up a chart describing those activities that the caregiver can use to support and encourage the child's emotional, physical, and cognitive growth.

In Elizabeth, New Jersey, head teacher Kathy Santor does developmental screening for each child every two months, using the Denver Screening and the Hawaiian Screening. She then meets with each child care worker weekly to discuss what they have observed in their children—whether they seem advanced or delayed, according to expectations derived from the testing. Kathy Santor also devotes time each week to work with each group of children on a specific aspect of development: for example, acquiring gross or fine motor skills.

In another center where a large percentage of incoming infants have been found to have delayed development, the head teacher designs a plan for each child, using the Batelle and Bergance Assessment scales. The mother is counselled to understand the plan's learning objectives and to practice assigned exercises at home. She is also asked to contribute her own goals for her child, which can be built into the plan. When there is a severe amount of delay in a child, the teacher brings in a diagnostician from the local child study center. The parent is included in this assessment.

Individualized plans can be designed without using formal scales. However, formal scales are a useful tool to indicate how effectively the program is meeting children's needs and may be incorporated to measure outcomes in the center's evaluation plan.

Keeping records

Keeping individual records is useful for many purposes. Therefore, time must be allotted at the end of the day for teachers to record their observations. Many centers provide a checklist to teachers for charting the development of children. Items are checked at the end of each day or week, also following consultations with the mother. Progress reports for each child are completed on a periodic basis. With this approach, the role of a head teacher becomes pivotal. He or she becomes responsible for gathering each teacher's observations into the child's file, assessing progress, and encouraging additional individualized approaches if they are necessary. Children who appear to be falling behind are given special attention or referred for medical examination or further formal assessment.

Keeping careful records of staff observations concerning each child's progress over time is helpful for documenting the program's effectiveness. Administrators will want to assess the impact of the program's interventions, and funding sources want to be sure that the program is meeting its objectives. Both purposes demand comprehensive documentation of improvement in the children's cognitive, emotional, and physical development.

Cheryl Dyle, in St. Louis, believes that it is vital for program planners to begin by identifying measurable outcomes for success. Using formal pre- and post-testing and keeping detailed individual records will enable the program to document its success in meeting targeted outcomes and in alleviating delayed development, even in early stages of implementation.

Activity areas

Child care centers often divide their space into activity areas. The Center for Infant Development in Elizabeth has areas for sleeping, arts and crafts, music, manipulative play, and larger toys. Each teacher is responsible for a group of four children of the same age, and the groups rotate around the center, spending half an hour or so in each area.

The following seven areas are suggested by Jennifer Birckmayer and Anne Willis in *Guidelines for Day Care Programs for Migrant Infants and Toddlers*:

Book and story-telling area. Constant exposure to books and stories is important to a child's growth long before the child is able to read. A comfortable area with a bright, washable rug and pillows provides a setting for children to look at books alone or with staff and for storytelling activities. Books are best displayed facing out on a low bookshelf, about a dozen at a time.

Music area. Equipment for this area consists of a variety of simple, safe instruments, kept within easy reach of children, and a record player and records (or cassette deck and cassettes) stored out of reach. If space is limited, this area can be combined with the book and storytelling area.

Housekeeping and dramatic-play area. Dramatic play often provides a context for the emergence of social relationships as well as language development and use of imagination. Common features are a sturdy play stove, sink, shelves, doll beds large and strong enough for children as well as dolls, a low table, and several chairs. Accessories are crucial in this area and may include doll- or regular-sized plastic dishes; pots and pans; rubber dolls and their high chairs, carriages, and clothes; empty food containers (with no sharp edges); sponges and an empty dishwashing liquid container; a toy telephone; dress-up clothes; and a full-length mirror. If real water is used, clean-up equipment should be close at hand. Many centers cover the floor of this area with oilcloth or linoleum.

Block area. This area provides a rich assortment of materials for children to stack or build as well as opportunities for development of skills later needed for reading and mathematics. Children learn from staff to distinguish and compare shapes and sizes. A guideline when planning this area is to choose materials that can be used in many different ways. Prices for blocks may seem high, but they are a good investment, and a community or merchants' group may be persuaded to buy them for the center. Students in high school woodworking classes might be willing to make blocks or other materials for the center. Suggested purchases to complement the blocks include large sets of sturdy rubber (not wooden) animals that stand up; small wooden, rubber, or metal cars, trucks, trains, and planes; and large ride-on trucks with rubber wheels (wooden are too loud in a group). Scraps such as paper towel tubes, short lengths of hose, and pieces of cardboard can also add to variety. This area needs a sturdy, well-balanced storage unit of low shelves, so that children can see sizes and shapes and can help put blocks away.

Art area. Painting, play dough, pasting, fingerpainting, and stringing large macaroni are all possible. Activities should be age-appropriate—some materials can be used safely by two-year-olds but not one-year-olds. Plans should be made for clean-up when the area is designed. Smocks can be made from old shirts with the sleeves cut off. When weather permits, art activities can be transferred outside.

Large muscle area. Equipment for jumping and climbing is essential for large muscle development. An old mattress or large cushions can be of use here, especially when the weather prohibits outside play. Depending on scheduling, accessibility, and safety concerns, it may be possible to arrange to use part of the high school gymnasium for vigorous play, if the center itself has limited space.

Small muscle area. Puzzles, sorting and stacking toys, and other manipulative games are important in small muscle development. These materials can be stored on low shelves with a child-sized table and chairs nearby for play.

Equipment and materials
The following criteria for selecting equipment and materials for toddlers are useful.

All equipment should be simple, durable, scaled to the physical comfort of the children (chairs six to eight inches from the floor, tables ten to twelve inches), be well designed (no sharp edges or pinch places), safe, and, if painted, painted with lead-free paint. Remember that materials that are safe for older two-year-olds are not necessarily safe for young one-year-olds. Children are very interested in items associated with adults, like pots and pans, dress-up clothes, jewelry, tools. Small pieces of these items, however, can be dangerous to very young children.

All individual pieces of equipment should be purchased as part of a total program plan. Care must be taken to assemble a variety of toys with a variety of educational purposes. Toys that encourage children to make things and to imagine them are important. For example, a simple truck that can be sat on or loaded with blocks is preferable to a fancy wind-up car that can be used in only one way. A plain rubber doll that can be dressed and washed is preferable to a rag doll with stitched-on clothes. Opportunities for sand and water play are essential for older toddlers who have moved beyond the eating-sand stage!

Large equipment for experimental climbing, crawling, jumping, and such are useful. Cars to ride and baby carriages to push provide great amusement. Gyms and swing sets are wonderful for older toddlers but can be unsafe for younger toddlers. If you can replace hard swing seats with tires or canvas sling seats, do so, because toddlers are likely to run or back into a moving swing. Teeter-totters or see-saws must be closely supervised, as one toddler is quite likely to get off suddenly, leaving his or her partner to fall to the ground abruptly.

CHAPTER SEVEN
Programming for Mothers

The challenges inherent in providing young children with a developmentally sound child care program are magnified when the parents of these children are teenagers. In effect, center staff simultaneously serve two groups of youngsters at the opposite ends of childhood—infants and adolescents.

The challenge of serving two types of clients is further complicated by the life situations of the student mothers. Most mothers using these centers are trying to:

- meet family responsibilities as well as education requirements;
- cope with the usual ups and downs of adolescence while making decisions about the future that are both more serious and more circumscribed because of their parenting obligations;
- handle the various problems that plague young women from families or neighborhoods struggling with economic instability;
- develop a positive relationship with a new husband or with the baby's father; and
- pursue living arrangements that ensure financial security.

The responsibilities facing young mothers are formidable. Therefore, on the one hand, student mothers need support—attention, care, concrete assistance, and reassurance. On the other hand, these mothers need guidance around parenting practices, vocational preparation, personal relationships, and women's issues. In short, staff have to be prepared to *nurture and nag*.

The tensions for staff in trying to manage multiple roles toward student mothers are often exacerbated by the mothers' responses toward the staff. Of course, many mothers have the personal maturity to simply blossom in an environment that is more personal and caring. Other mothers prosper, but the social or emotional deprivation of their lives also leads them to set up staff, either individually or collectively, as parental surrogates with whom they can act out various conflicts. For example, a staff member may be perceived as the longed-for "good parent," which can lead to dependency behavior or inappropriate demands for contact. Or staff members may be viewed as adequate but disappointing in that they will not give enough; and this can lead to rebellion or detachment.

In summary, working with mothers *and* babies is a complex undertaking. The next section of this chapter offers suggestions for programming that will allow you to further refine your work with teen mothers and their children to meet their particular needs more precisely and successfully. The experiences and recommendations included here reflect the judgment of service providers on what works best.

Wisdom from the field

Staff at the centers we surveyed were especially eager to provide examples of the myriad ways they responded to the specific needs of teenage mothers. They stressed the wastefulness of allowing new programs to reinvent the wheel. In offering these suggestions, center staff were justifiably proud of being responsive and inventive. They also included recommendations that would help staff maintain their sensitivity and skills with young mothers.

What follows are the top tips from a number of experts who are pros at the delivery of services to teenage mothers and their children.

Assist teen mothers in establishing peer-support networks. Try to squeeze some time from students' schedules so they can meet as a group with some center staff. Use this time for training or other sorts of group activities—group activities that enhance a sense of group solidarity and strengthen peer support networks. Solicit contributions or freebies from local businesses or groups to support this approach. Consider getting tee shirts for kids and their moms. Let the mothers decide what should be printed on the shirts. Distribute "baby books" and encourage mothers to write their observations of their child's behavior and their own feelings about being a mother. Structure time when mothers can read aloud to each other from their books. Distribute personal calendars, then plan a group event and help mothers learn how to develop and record a schedule for themselves.

Provide training for young mothers through learn-by-doing approaches. Avoid lectures and too much teacher-talk. Develop learning activities that are fun and then make the most of the "teachable moments" you generate. Make child development concepts real for young mothers by providing each of them with a daily written report on their child's day. Keep your remarks short, specific, and concrete. In subsequent reports and conversations, reinforce ideas you have introduced. Always try to emphasize the positive.

Offer concrete ways for student mothers to develop positive parenting practices. Encourage mothers to practice alternative ways of handling difficult situations with their children by doing role plays with each other. Set up one mother with a file card on which you write instructions for how to proceed. Allow mothers to explore their reactions to that approach as well as alternative approaches offered by the other mothers. Reinforce your points with handouts—cartoons, catchy phrases, and the like. Expect that many young mothers will have very limited notions about how to help a child develop self-control and cooperative relationships with others. Mothers will want to know how to discipline children so they will mind. Have staff read Rudolf Dreikurs' *Children: The Challenge* and develop positive ways in which to help mothers learn to help their children. Remember you must always model what you are teaching.

Use many approaches to reinforce basic themes in your program. Select particular themes or catchy phrases that are a high priority for your center and repeat this material frequently in a variety of settings. Consider, for example, the impact of a large sign in your center that asks: "Does your home meet the 3S test? We want every one of our children in a *safe, stimulating, secure environment!*"

Address family planning issues repeatedly with participants. Offer frequent opportunities for student mothers to discuss matters related to family planning. Make sure the mother has a health practitioner she likes for birth control services. Develop a variety of strategies for reinforcing the notion that the next baby should be deferred and planned.

Involve participants' families in program activities. Organize social functions where grandparents and partners can attend, tour the center, and learn about your ideas.

Structure regular meetings for staff development and communication. Provide staff with adequate opportunities to explore the worldview of mothers who are more difficult to help (or troublesome in other ways) and to examine alternative ways to work with each of them. Many centers call these "case management conferences." Set aside time for staff to discuss parent–child interactions (as observed in your center) for each young mother you serve. Determine who will work with each mother on helping her improve her parenting skills. Make sure your interactions with the mothers are frequent and encouraging. Above all, approach her in ways that *build upon her strengths* as a mother.

Recruiting participants

Recruiting participants for child care centers is usually based on referrals from school personnel, especially guidance counselors. Referrals may also come from other service personnel, such as hospital or clinic workers, public or school nurses, or social workers. Centers in cities, such as Elizabeth and Fort Worth, which operated separate schools for pregnant teens, conducted promotional sessions at those schools. Students at Rule High School, Knoxville, find out about the center through high school home economics courses in child care, held in conjunction with center staff. Announcements are also made over the school's loudspeaker system. Some centers, such as Bay Ridge LYFE Program, have received a considerable amount of media coverage and are contacted by more than enough student mothers acting on their own initiative.

The amount of recruiting a center needs to do will depend on center capacity and the concentration of its target population. If the need in the center's vicinity is sufficient to fill the center, then recruiting outside of the local high school is wasteful of staff efforts and unfair to those that must be turned away. The center at Murray-Wright has been in existence for some years. High school teachers and guidance counselors know about the center and publicize it by word of mouth. Neighborhood demand is high enough that, through these informal channels, the center receives more applicants than it can handle.

A new center may have to take more aggressive measures to recruit participants, especially if student mothers have tended to drop out of school after delivery. The director may have to elicit referrals. Information may have to be disseminated through the professional network in other high schools of close proximity and in appropriate social welfare agencies. Wider recruiting efforts will be limited by the center's location and the convenience of transportation.

Recruiting the participation of mothers who have already dropped out of high school is more difficult and requires a more comprehensive community network. The center at Vashon High School, St. Louis, is subsumed under Parent/Infant Interaction Program, which has a standard citywide recruitment process. Adolescent mothers are informed of the various services offered by PIIP through a sustained publicity campaign and are referred to the center, if it is appropriate to their needs. PIIP also has an extensive referral and record-keeping system across community high schools aimed at keeping track of pregnant and parenting adolescents.

Informational materials describing your center's goals, hours, fees, program, target population, and registration procedures will be necessary. Make them simple and appealing.

Formal educational objectives for parents

All centers consider the successful completion of high school to be the primary educational objective for teen mothers. Some centers, however, develop formal education plans for the mothers and focus on their programs accordingly. The Preschool/Parenting Learning Center follows the educational targets listed below. Through various program features and components the participating mothers are to increase their understanding of:

- the center's philosophy and operating procedures (for example, the use of records/charts, individual daily program for children, rules, safety procedures, and opportunities for observation of the children);
- child development (for example, physical and mental developmental stages);
- infant care skills (for example, feeding, bathing, clothing, diaper changing);
- encouraging healthy emotional development (for example, through use of a flexible daily schedule, through approaches that foster positive self-esteem, through use of positive reinforcement, through helping toddlers develop and use words for their feelings);
- child stimulation activities (for example, issues related to play spaces, toys, out-of-doors play);
- toddler care skills (for example, how to encourage verbal development, "babyproofing," television program monitoring, toilet training);
- nutrition (for example, by exploring appropriate topics, such as the four food groups, prenatal nutrition, breast feeding, bottle feeding, and formulas); and
- community resources (for example, emergency contacts, family planning, health and social services).

Meeting such educational targets may be the responsibility of the center or the joint responsibility of the center and the high school. The latter case requires close collaboration among the center director, the advisory board, and the high school principal. In this instance, you will want to collectively design a strategy that incorporates structured parental participation in the center, individual and group education at the center, referrals to other service providers, and enrollment in regular high school courses. The right mix will depend on characteristics of the site, the level of school district support, and available resources.

Joint program planning can be administratively taxing. The school board may have to formally approve additional activities, requiring renewed lobbying among support groups and policymakers. Relations with the school's administrative and teaching staffs become more complicated. Courses offered through or in conjunction with the center have to be fit into the school's schedule and curriculum and be designated credits. Supportive services may require separate administrative and funding structures. In addition, the center may want to involve other agencies in its program, sharing tasks and responsibilities through referral. Then the director's liaison duties will be substantially increased.

Structured center participation

The easiest and most cost-effective way to incorporate mothers in a center's operations is to have them participate in feeding, caring for, and playing with their infants. Participation may be voluntary or required, depending on the mother's course load and the flexibility of scheduling within the high school. Where schedules are more rigid, mothers are asked to volunteer an agreed-upon number of hours per week, in time slots that do not interfere with their studies. Where schedules are more flexible, centers mandate a minimum time requirement for participation, usually ten to fifteen hours per week. Mothers are expected to sign in with their children, spend their lunch hour in the center, and sign out immediately after classes are completed. Sign-in and sign-out may include a daily report form or a brief consultation with teachers concerning the child's day. Participation during lunch hours allows a more structured exposure to the center's purpose and program. Mothers can be assigned to specific staff members and assist with the care of other infants in addition to their own. Allowing expanded, supervised responsibilities in this manner serves to reinforce principles of child care, which the mother can use to interact with her child away from the center.

Each center should review its own circumstances when establishing policies regarding the mothers' involvement in the center. At the Center for Infant Development in Elizabeth, New Jersey, mothers must spend two lunches a week at the center, and they are encouraged to come to the center at other times as well. Mothers are welcome during study hall if their grades are adequate. At the Polytechnic Center mothers are required to spend all of their lunches at the center, where they feed their children and interact with staff.

In contrast, the LYFE center's policy is for mothers to come in only before school with their children and to return for them after school. This policy grew from the belief that the mothers should be concentrating on their schooling during the day and not on their children.

However interaction is structured, most centers agree that, where space permits, mothers should be allowed access to the center when it is convenient for them. The more they are exposed to the center's routines and the more confidence they have in its staff, the more they will feel comfortable discussing appropriate approaches and emulating the staff.

Although participation by fathers in a center's daily program is usually desired, it rarely occurs on a consistent basis. Many fathers are inhibited by social and cultural factors. If the father is not married to his child's mother, he may feel uncomfortable about proclaiming his role as father. Even if he is married, child care may be seen to conflict with a manly persona that a young man feels compelled to adopt through upbringing or peer pressure. These attitudes are slow to change.

A receptive father who is enrolled in the high school should be encouraged to take part in caring for his child, to take parenting courses, or to attend other education sessions. Such participation can be presented as responsible parent behavior rather than male or female role-specific.

Most center staff stressed that they felt it was extremely important to include any interested fathers in as many center activities as possible. They recognized the need to reinforce the desirability of the father–child bond.

Parent education

Parent education is both a formal and an informal pursuit. Parent education is enhanced by the staff's example as role models. Each time a mother enters the center, she observes staff members interacting with her child in ways that might be different from her own. Teachers also function as consultants to the mother and sometimes other members of her family or the child's father. For example, an experienced caregiver can help a mother develop more realistic expectations for her child by commenting informally and frequently on the child's behavior and progress. As teachers are obligated to share their experiences and observations with mothers on a regular basis, they are able to respond to a mother's feelings, observations, or concerns and affect changes in her treatment of her child. Effective parent education depends on the *relationship* between mother and teacher.

Informal parent education can be reinforced by formal approaches. Almost all centers have rules that address discipline practices. For example, the Murray-Wright Infant–Toddler Center instructs parents on "positive methods of discipline which encourage the development of self-control, self-direction, self-esteem and cooperation." Parents are encouraged to discuss discipline questions or problems with center staff. Mothers are not allowed to hit a child or raise their voices in the center.

Parent education is best viewed as providing information, counseling, and guidance. Through these efforts, the parenting role is more clearly defined. Equally important, mothers learn that knowing how to be a good parent is an acquired skill—one that takes time, practice, mistakes, and a willingness to go on learning.

During the first years, especially, parents need a great deal of practical information just to cope with the responsibilities of caring for an infant and toddler. As the child grows, the parent's understanding of cognitive, social, and emotional issues must also grow.

A parent education curriculum that focuses on the many ways a center can foster a mother's parenting skills is far more likely to be successful than approaches that focus almost exclusively on instructing mothers.

Relevant high school courses

More formal parent education can be provided through classes offered through the high school. Classes are typically offered through the school's home economics and health departments, and topics include family life, nutrition, and child development.

Sample daily report form

Child's name _____ Date _____

Parent's name _____ Caregiver's name _____

	To be filled out in morning by parent.	**To be filled out by caregiver.**
Mood	Describe child's mood at home.	Describe child's mood at center.
Health	Describe child's health. Medication: _____ Dosage: _____ Time last given: _____ _____	Describe child's health. Medication: _____ Dosage: _____ Time last given: _____
Food	What did child eat for breakfast? Time: _____	What did child eat at center? Time: _____
Bottles	Indicate type of bottles and time given.* Time: _____ _____ _____ Circle one: M J W M J W M J W *M Stands for milk, J stands for juice, and W stands for water.	Indicate type of bottles and time given.* Time: _____ _____ _____ Circle one: M J W M J W M J W *M Stands for milk, J stands for juice, and W stands for water.
Diapers/ Toilet	Indicate special diapering instructions. Does child have diarrhea? _____ Constipation? _____	Indicate time and type of diapering. Dry: _____ Dry: _____ Wet: _____ Wet: _____ BM: _____ BM: _____
Sleep	Did child sleep well last night? _____ When did child wake up? _____ When should child take nap? _____	When did child take nap? _____
Special comments		

Mothers in the LYFE program at Bay Ridge High School are required to take a credit-bearing class that provides instruction in nutrition, health education, and child development. This class meets daily for 45 minutes. Although this class is a requirement for mothers enrolled in the program, it can also be taken as an elective by nonprogram participants. The class is taught by a teacher on the school payroll who is trained in both child care and child development. Teachers discuss the physical, cognitive, and social development of infants and toddlers, treating such issues as the proper way to hold, change, and feed an infant; how to select children's toys, furniture, and clothing safely; how to deal with a child's negative behavior without resorting to physical punishment; and how to stimulate children's development through games and reading. In addition to these basic topics, the teacher also covers such topics as human reproductive systems, menstruation, early signs of pregnancy, and the techniques of medical supervision during and after pregnancy. Some teachers emphasize consumer awareness and nutrition, such as how to make nutritious and inexpensive baby foods at home. Class participants spend one period per week in the center, observing and assisting.

At the Crib Infant Care Center, teen mothers are required to take three life skills courses: (1) Parenting Skills (which includes a practicum in the center as well as opportunities to observe other adults with their children and to watch a teacher administer the Denver Screening Assessment), (2) Family Life Education (which focuses on topics such as dating and marriage), and (3) Career Education.

Group meetings

Organizing an ongoing group for program participants can be useful for disseminating parental education information and helping mothers develop peer support networks that will outlive their participation in the program. Group meetings may be formally structured around relevant topics with assigned educational materials for each unit. Films, guest speakers, visual aids, and demonstrations may also be used. Mothers should be involved in setting the agenda for the group, invited to share their experiences with one another, encouraged to practice skills, and urged to ask questions. Some meetings should be devoted to more personal topics that affect the students' capacity to do their best as parents. For example, groups often discuss their home lives and the reaction of family, partners, or husbands to their participation in the program.

Meetings may be led by program staff, by high school teachers, or by other professionals who are part of the program's referral network. Professionals are often willing to volunteer their time to direct such a group, or payment can be arranged through a variety of sources.

At Murray-Wright High School's center, parent groups initially met twice a month. Attendance at these meetings averaged well above 50 percent of those enrolled. Those not at the meeting because of work or other obligations received information from the teacher or assistants the next day. Meetings were generally concerned with discussing the stages of child growth and development and with school and community resources available for adolescent parents. Parents were so involved with these meetings that the school incorporated meeting content into an Adult Education class and assumed financial and curriculum obligations.

The Parent/Infant Interaction Program in St. Louis sponsors Prenatal Groups, which meet once a week for twelve to fourteen weeks, and Parenting Groups, which meet once a week for twenty weeks, to provide peer group support for adolescents. Both groups encourage frank discussion and open sharing of common problems and solutions. Meetings are organized around topics, such as parenting skills, techniques for handling children's negative behavior, sexuality and family planning, child abuse, and community resources. The importance of completing high school is continually stressed. PIIP also sponsors a Grandparents Support Group. Through participation in this group, parents of teen parents receive information and counseling to cope with the complex needs of adolescent pregnancy and parenting. All meetings are conducted by program staff or other professional volunteers.

Individual counseling

Center experiences suggest that the valuable role of groups should be augmented by some form of individual counseling and consultation, if resources permit. Often, a teenage mother will not want to discuss certain topics in a group, or she may have difficulty setting aside a specific block of time every week for a regularly scheduled meeting. Therefore, individual counseling provides a more private and more flexible alternative. Many program counselors have an open door policy, allowing the adolescent mother to come in and talk whenever she has a problem or during posted office hours. In St. Louis, the Parent/Infant Interaction Program Coordinator serves as advisor for most of the pregnant and parenting teens in Vashon High School. As such, she counsels the students regarding attendance, course scheduling, achievement tests, and special services.

A staff member-as-counselor should be prepared to discuss a wide variety of topics. He or she should be skillful in helping mothers sort out emotional issues and make decisions for the future. Such counseling can be handled initially by program staff. Referral to other professionals, such as a social worker, a nurse, a psychologist, or a school guidance counselor may be necessary if a mother needs more intensive psychological assistance.

Mentoring

Mentoring offers another approach to individualized counseling. The Ft. Worth YWCA, which operates the Polytechnic Child Care Center, found that it takes more than parent education courses to really help parents get the life skills they need. One successful approach has been their Mentor Program, which provides each girl with a role model, a volunteer who has attended a one-day intensive training session. Mentors are encouraged to remain in the program for a sustained period of time. Stephanie Rorie, executive director of the YWCA, cites the biggest problem with the program as mentors who are very involved initially and then drop off.

Referral services

The theory of referral is simple: any problems that fall beyond the scope of center time, resources, and expertise are referred to other specialists. However, organizing an efficient referral system can be difficult. It requires a detailed understanding of federal and state programs, bureaucratic channels, and personal contact with individuals who can direct a mother through what appears to be a laybrinth. The staff must understand the kinds of assistance programs that are available to young mothers and act as their advocate in receiving this assistance. This may require walking through the steps with young mothers, filling in and filing forms, knocking at the same doors week after week, and talking to the same people so often that you hear "Here comes Margie from the center again!" When it reaches this point, the referral network has begun to solidify.

Referrals are made for health-related problems, public assistance problems (budget adjustments, food stamps, WIC, or Medicaid), housing, education, and employment. To establish community contacts for each of these problem areas, go back over your list of community resources developed in the initial planning process, talk to those who have been helpful in the past, find out the names of those people likely to be useful to you, and meet with them. In most centers, unless a program has considerable resources, the director's office becomes the referral liaison office.

In New York, each LYFE program center is assigned one social worker and a family assistant. The social worker spends a good deal of time visiting the homes of student mothers and accompanying them to clinic appointments. She sees herself as an advocate for services to which these adolescents are entitled but of which they may be unaware. She collaborates with other staff members, offering relevant workshops to mothers. She approaches the task of aiding mothers on a very individualized basis, conducting an estimated 650 interviews, four per school day with the eighteen students at her site. She made an average of about six referrals to various community and government agencies per participant for the year.

Medical referrals are an essential part of every program. Adolescent mothers often need assistance in obtaining timely medical care. The program director should make every effort to establish formal links with community health resources. These should include arrangements with private physicians, with clinics, and with a nearby hospital, to provide "privileged" care for program participants. Most young mothers are eligible for financial assistance through Medicaid or other federal programs, and the director should intervene to ensure that all forms are properly filled out and filed and that their conditions are honored by medical practitioners.

Parent/Infant Interaction Program

As an illustration of how these various approaches to solid programming for student mothers work together as a whole, it is useful to describe the multifaceted Parent/Infant Interaction Program, which now includes the Crib Infant Care Center, as it was implemented in St. Louis.

The program was designed to meet the needs of participants with a differing mix of services in five phases.

Phase one: Intake. This phase addressed the needs of pregnant adolescents from the time of enrollment until the sixth month of pregnancy. Pregnant adolescents were referred to the program by schools, clinics, churches, and community organizations or were enrolled by direct contact initiated through program publicity. Program staff then provided further referrals to appropriate health and social service agencies and provided follow-up contact by telephone and personal interview. At this stage, one-to-one counseling was provided that included personal support, reinforcement of a positive self-concept, and teaching problem-solving strategies.

Phase two: Prenatal. After the sixth month of pregnancy, participants were encouraged to take part in peer support groups, composed of ten to fifteen girls with comparable estimated delivery dates. These groups met weekly, in the day or evening, and covered topics such as prenatal development, labor and delivery, family planning, and the care of newborns.

Phase three: Delivery and post partum. Support during labor and delivery were provided, if necessary. After delivery, mothers were visited at the hospital or at home by a program social worker. During these visits, mothers were recruited into the postnatal phase of the program. Other mothers, who had not participated in earlier phases, could enroll in the program at this time.

Phase four: Postnatal. Peer group sessions for mothers and their infants began three to five weeks after delivery and met weekly for twenty weeks. Groups were composed of ten to fifteen mother/infant pairs matched by infant age. Information covering child development from birth to one year, parenting skills, family planning, and referral to appropriate community agencies were provided in these meetings.

Phase five: Termination. In this phase, weekly sessions were discontinued, and an assessment of the mother's and infant's needs was made by program staff. In addition, guidance in planning for the future and in maintaining a support system for the family was offered.

Three years after implementing this program, a number of factors indicated the need for additional services. These included: a tripling of enrollment; the fact that not all young women were interested in group sessions; and a list of other information needs expressed by participants. To meet these newly identified needs, the program added individualized counseling for those who preferred it, added more education topics, and instituted a more extensive telephone follow-up process and more stringent school attendance monitoring. In response to increasing numbers of referrals with older children, the program took steps to extend the termination time and add a further phase of service. Today the program receives an average of 250 referrals per year, which are handled by a program staff consisting of four full-time counselors, one half-time administrative position, volunteers, and student interns. The program's components include systematic recruiting, on-site child care, peer support groups, health and social services referrals, home visitations, follow-up rotation calls, and school attendance monitoring.

CHAPTER EIGHT

The Center as a Learning Lab

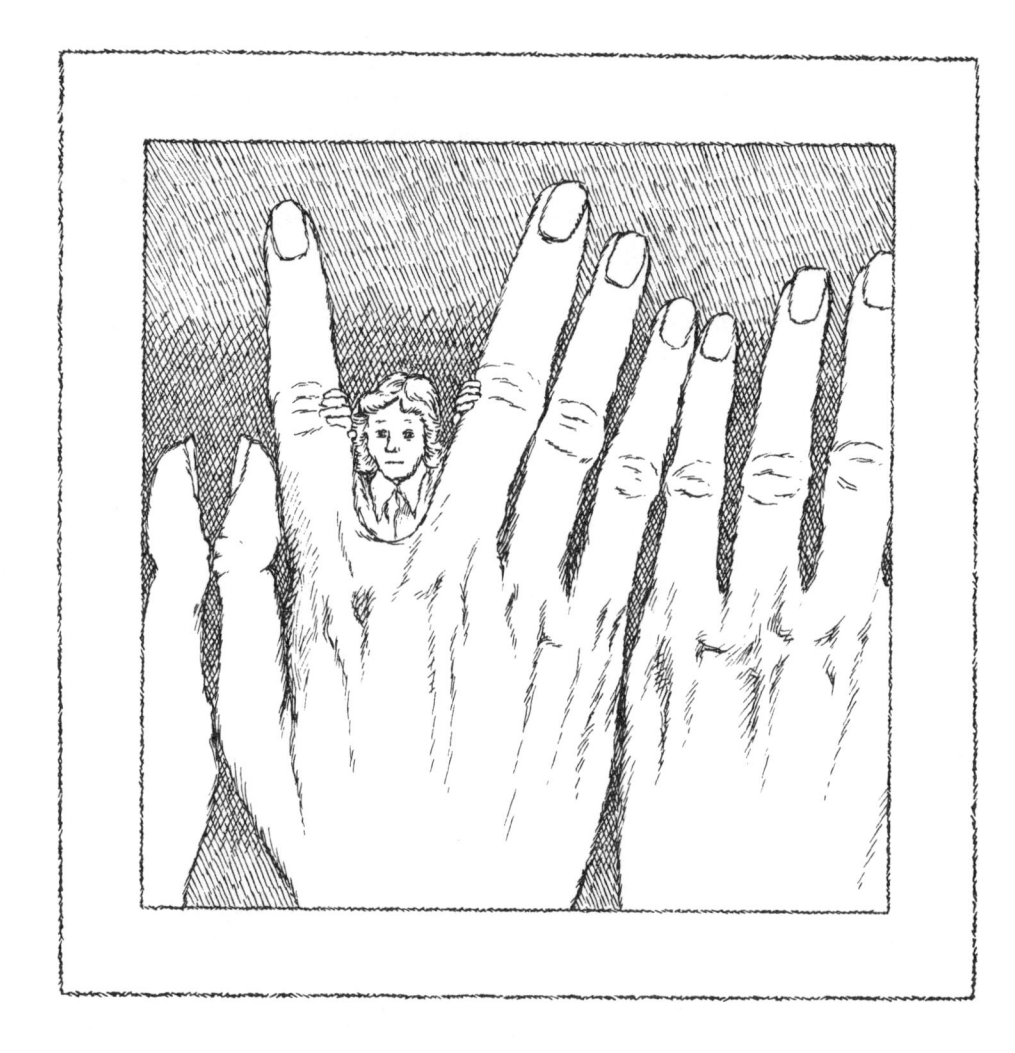

Programs such as Murray-Wright that serve as sites for course work or that offer vocational training are known as laboratory centers. Such centers offer high school students a chance to study child development or an opportunity to train for work in the area of child care services. Since they are an extensive undertaking, it is important that they be designed into the program at the beginning and seen as a primary objective of the center. If the learning lab approach is taken merely to build support for a child care center, planners will find themselves with far greater program demands than anticipated in their original concept. This model works well in some schools because it meets real objectives. In others it would be an artificial add-on.

The objectives for occupational training in child care set by the Murray-Wright Child Care Training Laboratory and Infant–Toddler Center are illustrative:

- to provide exploratory experiences with the preschool child to stimulate interest in child care services occupations;
- to provide the opportunity to develop an awareness of the needs of preschool children and to gain empathy, understanding, and a sense of responsibility when caring for them;

- to provide information about employment opportunities, limitations, and responsibilities in the child care services; and
- to provide sufficient practical experiences so that the students acquire basic skills necessary to perform some of the tasks required by various child care institutions.

Trainees who are not parents provide valuable labor for the center. Also, their observations of children and their mothers can be helpful to center staff since they are taught to think critically, to assimilate child development concepts, and to relate these concepts to practical child caring situations. Moreover, they are often peers of the student mothers and therefore especially insightful about their predicament.

Upon satisfactory completion of a child care curriculum, trainees in one program were expected to:
- analyze the critical factors in childbirth;
- apply accepted methods of child care in the center;
- understand the responsibilities of a child care assistant;
- identify developmental areas of infants and toddlers;
- describe the elements of good nutrition;
- plan play and learning experiences for children;
- critique educational materials;
- evaluate the safety and suitability of toys;
- demonstrate necessary first-aid techniques; and
- demonstrate an understanding of center safety procedures.

Many educators note that these skills, when properly taught, are easily transferred into a post-secondary program. It is important to develop curricula that challenge students to improve their basic academic skills, including reading, writing, and decision making. Students should be encouraged to understand the opportunities in the whole field—teaching, child psychology, and so forth—so that they do not limit themselves to entry-level jobs, which in the child care field have a low wage scale. Community colleges or universities with extensive offerings in child care and social services are a good resource for technical assistance and other support, and a laboratory center can provide productive high school and college collaboration.

A laboratory curriculum is usually an integral part of the high school's course offerings and is handled through the vocational education department with cooperation of the center and other interested departments. Laboratory centers demand extensive cooperation among the high school principal, the faculty, and the center director, and these centers are often fully integrated into the school district's administrative and budgeting structure. Laboratory centers are also eligible for grants under state and federal vocational progams and thus can provide an alternative approach to funding a center.

Internships in child care

At some centers experience in child care is offered to students taking courses that provide opportunities for vocational exploration. At the Center for Infant Development, Elizabeth, New Jersey, students can be paid to work in the center for work-study credit.

* * *

If your center experiences periodic shifting of trainees or students, it will be an additional burden for staff. Fortunately, most staff report that they enjoy sharing their knowledge and skills and are not put off by the high turnover.

CHAPTER NINE

Site and Space

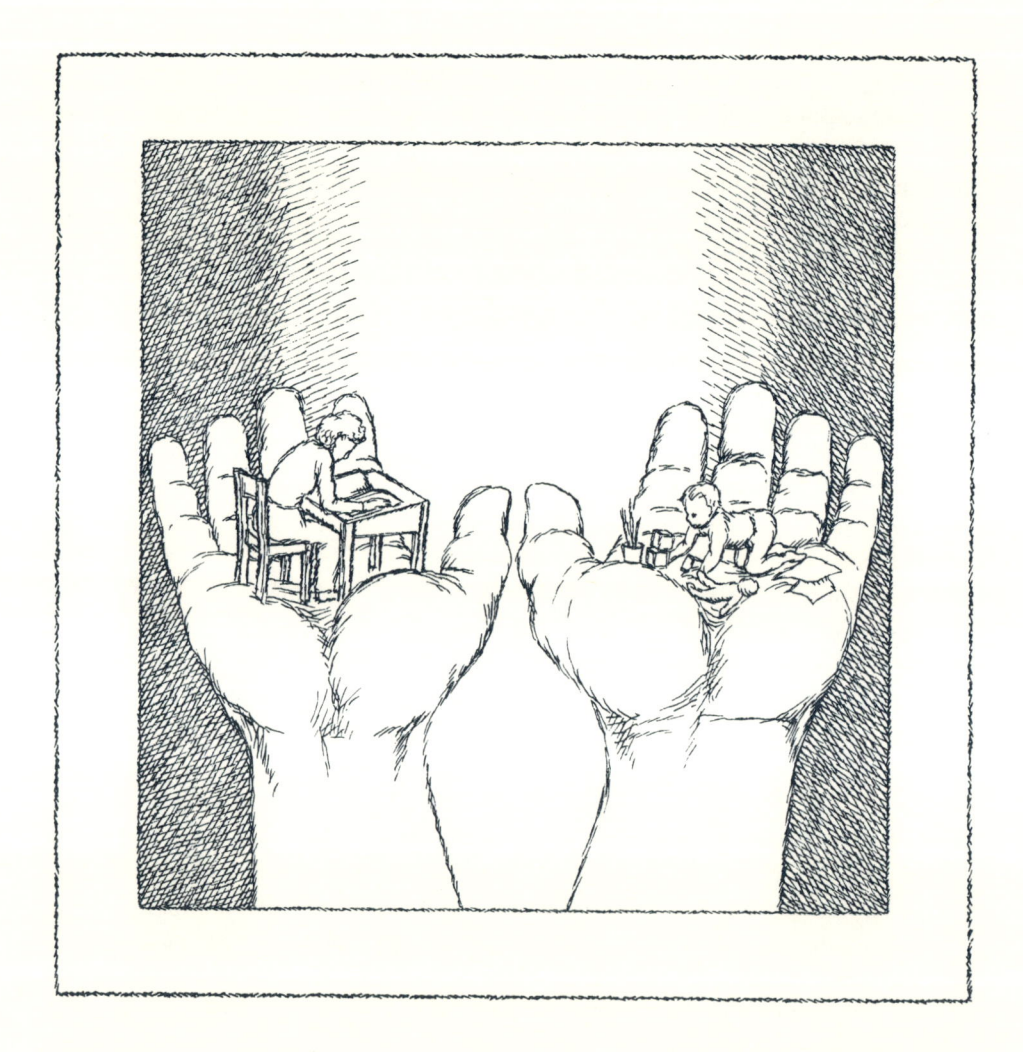

Child care centers operate successfully in a range of settings, from detached mobile trailers to renovated classrooms. Most staff members are convinced that the quality of personnel and content of programs are more influential in determining the success of operations than the location or quality of the space. "A well-designed program with good people can operate anywhere," said one respondent.

Typically, planners have a high school or neighborhood in mind for the center and must then work out the details of location and organization. The centers we surveyed appeared to follow certain common standards with respect to site and space, derived from child care studies, state and federal regulations, experience, and their focus on student mothers. Specific site selection and space organization is dependent on the needs of the target population, program objectives, available space, licensing requirements, and financial resources. Taken together, these considerations provide a framework of constraints that shape the planners' decision-making process.

Before the planners decide on a specific site for the child care center, the center's programs should be formally approved by the school board or other sponsoring agency. Letters of support, signed by all key decision makers, should be in the hands of planners. This requires planners to make a formal presentation before the school board or sponsoring agency's board of directors to detail objectives, program components, and anticipate expenses. If funding is being requested from the reviewing board, expect that there may be in-depth interrogation and a prolonged debate over many budget questions that may have nothing to do with child care. If funding is not expected from the board, then alternative funding strategies must be discussed and a funding proposal exhibited.

In a few cases, planners had already sought and been awarded funds from outside sources, provisional upon approval of the center. They used these monies to press for board approval and were successful. Money in the hand is effective evidence that a program's objectives are worthy of support. Most often, however, funding sources will want to know before awarding a grant that the program has already been approved by those agencies that might be able to veto its operations. Planners who have done their homework and are prepared to describe and defend the program they have designed have every reason to demand and expect support.

Licensing

Upon receipt of formal approval and commitments in writing, planners should move ahead with researching state and local licensing requirements. Public standards in the areas of safety, fire, health, building, sanitation, and so on will have to be adequately met by your center before it can open.

Call or make a personal visit to the licensing board to inform them of your intention to operate a child care center. Acquire copies of all applicable regulations. Determine what assistance is available from public agencies for complying with these regulations: this may include personal advisory assistance, handbooks, guidelines, or checklists. Visit or call the other offices that must grant approval. A school-based child care center may fall under overlapping jurisdictions, and it will take time-consuming negotiations to sort through them. Generally, states will not grant a license or will grant only a provisional license until planners can demonstrate that they can meet local as well as state codes.

Visit city and community officials to determine zoning requirements, building and fire codes, and any local ordinances that may deal specifically with the operation of child care centers. Zoning requirements for child care centers are often fuzzy—somewhere between residential and commercial, and special arrangements for a specific site may have to be negotiated with the city council or zoning board.

State and local officials are generally very helpful and supportive, but it is the nature of any bureaucracy to move slowly. Paperwork needs to be filed, hearings scheduled, and inspection visits arranged. Expect delays. It is best to keep all licensing authorities informed of program timetables and progress in meeting requirements on a regular basis. This ensures more personal attention and tends to eliminate "surprises" for both sides. The Crib Infant Care Center at Vashon High School issued monthly State Licensing Update Reports to all involved parties, detailing progress made in meeting requirements and listing what remained to be done.

Before deciding on a specific site or going ahead with renovations, be sure you are in compliance with the standards you will have to meet. You will waste precious program time and financial resources if you have to undo something or do it again.

Once you are set up, remember you will have to pass various inspections before you can officially open.

State child care center licensing offices*

Alabama
Office of Program Administration
64 North Union St., Montgomery, AL 36130

Alaska
Department of Health and Social Services
Pouch H-05, Juneau, AK 99811

Arizona
Department of Health Services
1740 West Adams, Phoenix, AZ 85007

Arkansas
Department of Social and Rehabilitative Services
P.O. Box 1487, Little Rock, AR 72203

California
Department of Social Services
744 P St., Mail Station 17-17, Sacramento, CA 95814

Colorado
Department of Social Services
1575 Sherman St., Room 420, Denver, CO 80203

Connecticut
State Department of Health
79 Elm St., Hartford, CT 06115

Delaware
Department of Health and Social Services
P. O. Box 309, Wilmington, DE 19899

District of Columbia
Licensing and Certification Division
Social Services Branch
1406 L St., N.W., Washington, D.C. 20005

Florida
Department of Health and Rehabilitation Services
1311 Winewood Blvd., Tallahassee, FL 32301

Georgia
Department of Human Services
618 Ponce de Leon Ave., Atlanta, GA 30308

Guam
Division of Social Services
P. O. Box 2816, Agana, Guam 96910

Hawaii
Department of Social Services and Housing
P. O. Box 339, Honolulu, HI 96809

Idaho
Department of Health and Welfare
Statehouse, Boise, ID 83720

Illinois
Department of Children and Family Services
1 North Old State Capitol Plaza, Springfield, IL 62706

Indiana
State Department of Public Welfare
100 North Senate Ave., Room 701,
Indianapolis, IN 46204

Iowa
Department of Social Services
3619½ Douglass Ave., Des Moines, IA 50310

Kansas
Division of Health and Environment
Building 740, Forbes AFB, Topeka, KS 66620

Kentucky
Department of Human Resources
275 East Main St., Frankfort, KY 40601

Louisiana
Department of Health and Human Resources
P. O. Box 3767, Baton Rouge, LA 70821

Maine
Department of Human Services
Augusta, ME 04333

Maryland
Department of Health and Mental Hygiene
201 West Preston St., Baltimore, MD 21201

Massachusetts
Office for Children
120 Boylston St., Boston, MA 02116

Michigan
Department of Social Services
116 West Allegan, P. O. Box 80037,
Lansing, MI 48926

Minnesota
Department of Public Welfare
Centennial Office Bldg., St. Paul, MN 55155

Mississippi
State Board of Health
P. O. Box 1700, Jackson, MS 39205

Missouri
State Department of Social Service
Broadway State Office Bldg., 303 West McCarthy St.
Jefferson City, MO 65103

Montana
Department of Social and Rehabilitative Services
P. O. Box 4210, Helena, MT 59601

Nebraska
Department of Public Welfare
P. O. Box 95026, Lincoln, NE 68509

*Reprinted from *Information Sheet #25*, Child Care Action Campaign, Fall 1985.

Nevada
Division of Youth Services
505 East King St., Carson City, NV 89710

New Hampshire
Office of Social Services
Hazen Dr., Concord, NH 03301

New Jersey
Department of Human Services
1 South Montgomery St., Trenton, NJ 08623

New Mexico
Health and Environment Department
440 Chamisa Hill Bldg., Suite S-3,
Santa Fe, NM 87501

New York
Department of Social Services
40 North Pearl St., Albany, NY 12243

New York City Agency for Child Development
240 Church St., New York, NY 10013

North Carolina
Office of Child Day Care Licensing
1919 Ridge Rd., Raleigh, NC 27607

North Dakota
Children and Family Services
Russell Bldg., Box 7, Highway 83 North
Bismarck, ND 58505

Ohio
Bureau of Licensing and Standards
30 East Broad St., Columbus, OH 43215

Oklahoma
Department of Public Welfare
P. O. Box 25352, Oklahoma City, OK 73125

Oregon
Department of Human Resources
198 Commercial St., S.E., Salem, OR 97310

Pennsylvania
Department of Public Welfare
Health and Welfare Bldg., Room 423,
Harrisburg, PA 17120

Puerto Rico
Department of Social Services
P. O. Box 11398, Fernandez Juncos Station
Santurce, PR 00910

Rhode Island
Department of Social and Rehabilitative Services
610 Mount Pleasant Ave., Providence, RI 02908

South Carolina
Department of Social Services
P. O. Box 1520, Columbia, SC 29202

South Dakota
Department of Social Services
Richard F. Kneip Bldg., Pierre, SD 57501

Tennessee
Department of Human Services
111-19 7th Avenue North, Nashville, TN 37203

Texas
Department of Human Resources
P. O. Box 2960, Austin, TX 78769

Utah
Division of Family Services
P. O. Box 2500, Salt Lake City, UT 84110

Vermont
Department of Social and Rehabilitative Services
81 River St., Montpelier, VT 05602

Virgin Islands
Department of Social Services
P. O. Box 539, Charlotte Amalie,
St. Thomas, VI 00801

Virginia
Department of Welfare
8007 Discovery Dr., Richmond, VA 23229

Washington
Department of Social and Health Services
State Office Bldg. #2, Mail Stop 440,
Olympia, WA 98504

West Virginia
Department of Welfare
1900 Washington St., East, Charleston, WV 25305

Wisconsin
Division of Community Services
1 West Wilson St., Madison, WI 53702

Wyoming
Division of Public Assistance and Social Services
Hathway Bldg., Cheyenne, WY 82002

Site selection

Selecting a specific site for a child care center involves basic considerations of accessibility, availability, and suitability.

Accessibility

One of the prime justifications for providing school-based child care is that the service is convenient for student mothers. Therefore, a center should be located where it is easily accessible. Of the six centers studied, all are located in or adjacent to a high school, where mothers using the center are enrolled. The physical proximity of the center reduces time and transportation demands and makes it easier for mothers to check in with their infants in the morning, then go on to classes. It also reduces daily operating hours, as check-in and check-out times can more closely mesh with school hours.

The center's objectives need to be considered when weighing the accessibility of a potential site. Simple child care may be provided conveniently within several blocks of the high school. However, if one of the center's objectives is to teach parenting skills or provide opportunities for mother–infant interaction throughout the day, then closer proximity is required. A laboratory center that involves nonparenting students in child care courses is usually located in the school or on school grounds. The more comprehensive the educational or vocational components of the program, the closer the center needs to be to auxiliary facilities, classrooms, and other users.

The Center for Infant Development in Elizabeth was originally housed in a mobile trailer some distance from the city's high school. In spite of the transportation complications, enrollment was maintained because few other program options existed. Over several years the center established itself as a permanent institution and secured greater community acceptance for its program. Community development funds were used to purchase the present site, which is in a former school building across the street from the main complex of Elizabeth High School. This move allowed the center to increase enrollment and expand services, a result of both improved proximity and enlarged space. Although the center is not in the building in which most mothers attend classes, the center worked with the high school to develop flexible scheduling to allow mothers to spend lunch hours with their children. They also made arrangements to coordinate mothers' schedules to allow them to attend group meetings.

In situations where the site has to be separate from the high school, the strategy, on the whole, appears to be to maximize mothers' participation by negotiating scheduling and transportation arrangements with the school.

Availability

Often, a choice of site will be a compromise between accessibility and availability. None of the centers studied owned its own property. Each was housed on school property or on property acquired by a community agency for the purpose of housing the center. Often the site was not the planning committee's first choice, yet the space was deemed adequate or the price acceptable. Purchasing or leasing a site is usually beyond the means of a child care center, particularly in the beginning, so the center makes itself dependent on sponsored or donated space. In this situation, the school board may select empty classrooms or an unused cafeteria; the city may offer to renovate an under-used recreational facility; a church might be willing to donate space as a part of its own community outreach programs; a local agency, such as the YWCA, may volunteer space in a neighborhood center.

Among several sites that are made available to the center the relative accessibility of each should be weighed, estimated costs of renovation compared, and institutional ties considered. In most cases, if the center's aim is incorporation into the school system, arrangements with the school board are preferred.

Sometimes the center may not have the luxury of choosing among sites but must take what is offered, whatever the trade-offs. Inaccessibility and inconvenience will limit enrollment and program options, but when choice is restricted, a decision may have to be made to begin with what is available and to relocate when the opportunity arises. Many centers have relocated three or four times, improving accessibility with each move. If only one site seems available, the planning committee should then think big, but start small, that is, retain the overall program design in theory but plan to implement only those objectives that can be accommodated by the site.

Suitability

The ideal child care center should be separate, on a first floor, and specifically designed for the purpose, with a private entrance just for program participants and with outdoor play space. This ideal setting is most suitable because it offers the following features:
- it is safe from hazards of stairwells and upper-story windows;
- it is easily evacuated in case of fire or other emergency;
- it allows individual access and egress, isolating infants and toddlers from disrupting crowds;
- it allows maximum supervision of children;
- it allows staff to regulate outside contact and provide a secure, homelike atmosphere within the center;
- it permits scheduling according to the needs of the children, rather than according to the schedules and demands of other building occupants; and
- it permits easy access to outdoor play areas.

According to these criteria, none of the centers visited were housed in an ideal space from inception. Centers with a separate building were often either in semipermanent trailers or mobile classrooms. Others were housed in multi-use buildings with varying degrees of insulation from surrounding activities, often sharing entrances with the school or a sponsoring agency, sharing play areas with other groups, or forced to schedule according to conflicting events. None of the spaces was originally designed for child care; all needed to be converted from a previous use. Building safety and fire codes sometimes precluded first choices.

For example, the Preschool/Parenting Learning Center in Knoxville was to provide vocational training for other students, as well as youth services for student mothers. It thus needed to be located in the school or on school grounds. During initial planning stages, an empty classroom in the high school was selected for the center, but the room did not meet building code requirements or fire inspection. At this point, a portable classroom building was acquired from another school and moved to the high school grounds to house the center. Extensive renovations were needed to fit the classroom for child care. The center gained a separate facility but lost in terms of time, expense, size of space, and permanence. The resulting arrangement was deemed the most adequate that could be devised and a decision made to go ahead with the temporary arrangement.

We found that centers established a list of ideal criteria as a goal yet displayed flexibility in approaching that goal. Priority was given to ensuring safety and sanitation for infants and toddlers, and to providing enough space for program activities.

Other criteria often had to be compromised but did not go unconsidered.

A determination of site adequacy will also rest on the amount of space available. Space allowance per infant and child is usually strictly specified in state licensing requirements and varies from state to state. Specifications typically require a minimum of 30 to 50 square feet of indoor play space and 50 to 80 square feet of outdoor play space per toddler or older child. Infant care requires from 25 to 50 square feet per infant. Therefore, the expected ratio of infants to toddlers will affect the amount of space needed.

In selecting a site you will want to add your own requirements to those made by public agencies. A child care center needs more than just rooms for children and a playground. While some centers operate successfully with less space than they need, they do so by restricting teachers' office, lounge, kitchen, or storage space, which often places undue hardships on teachers and administrators. Teachers need space, too, if they are to be organized.

If the program's objectives dictate extensive parent–child interaction, space allowances should be increased to prevent overcrowding. If your center is a laboratory school, it may need more space.

Going into a new space, center planners can easily underestimate the amount of space that center activities will require. They should also allow room, if possible, for expansion. Otherwise, increased enrollment may require finding and renovating an entirely different space.

As in all forms of bargaining, planners should set two space figures: a higher figure, which provides for more space than is technically required and allows for growth; and a lower figure, based on the necessary minimum. Be prepared to settle for a figure that falls somewhere in between.

The size of the center has surprisingly little bearing on economy of operations. The amount of space, number of staff, and equipment are tied with enrollment and must be increased in direct proportion to the number of children served.

Responsibility for locating a site

In most cases, the advisory board plays an essential role in locating a space that meets planning criteria and in arranging for its possession. In many ways, the board must work to influence availability by broadcasting the objectives and planning criteria to potential donors or sponsors.

Space renovations

The physical environment of an infant and toddler program is second in importance after the quality of its staff and design of its program. A well-designed space simplifies daily routines, makes supervision easier, improves center safety, and provides a range of different interest and activity areas for children. Space renovations should be based on sound principles of infant and child development and should reflect the changing needs of growing children and the needs of staff.

Often planners draw on their own experience to design a space themselves, rather than hiring an architect. Many work closely with a respected contractor. Extensive renovations, however, will probably require professional advice, and costs can be included in start-up expenses. In Elizabeth, the city provided in-kind architectural consultation and services for renovating the Center for Infant Development's space. Other centers received seed money through an initial funding proposal to cover these and other start-up expenses.

Issues in space organization

The remainder of this chapter discusses more general considerations for space organization—such as safety, health and sanitation, and comfort—that contribute to a sound and secure center environment.

Safety

The adults at the center are responsible for foreseeing and eliminating potential hazards for small children. Foresight begins when planning to renovate a space. For example, floor coverings should be smooth, splinterproof, and easily cleaned. Toddler areas should be carpeted to cushion the jolts of learning to walk. Stairs should be replaced with ramps in rooms with different floor levels and appropriate barricades provided. When possible, all rooms used by young children should be on a single-level ground floor. Some licensing codes even require it. If stairs must be used, banisters and gates should be provided and all open stairwells guarded. Windows and balconies need safety screens or bars that cannot be climbed on or through. Building exits should be equipped with childproof locks or doorknobs too high for the children to reach.

For protection against fire, each floor should have at least two widely separated exits; classroom and exit doors should open out. Upper-floor fire escapes should be of the shute type, usable by small children. A sprinkler system may be required by law and, even if it is not, should be considered. Smoke detectors and fire alarms are essential. Local fire regulations should be met and exceeded.

Electrical wiring needs minute inspection and replacement if it appears too old. Outlets should be sufficient to avoid any need for extension cords, and unused outlets covered. Heating and ventilation should be built-in to avoid the need for portable heaters and fans. Open gas flames of any type are usually restricted.

A safe space is one that is easily supervised. Safe area partitions divide the room visually for children but do not restrict an adult's range of vision. Unused areas are sealed off and locked. Exits should be within the view of some staff member at all times. Traffic patterns need to be plotted when separating quiet from active areas.

Outdoor play areas should be fenced and have good drainage to avoid standing water. Permanent playground equipment should be solidly built and free from sharp edges. Every point or protrusion will eventually claim a victim.

Health and sanitation

Neglecting proper sanitation is a major contributing factor to spreading infections. Take care that all surfaces are constructed of waterproof and easily cleaned materials, especially in food preparation areas. Kitchen fixtures should be built-in. Sewage disposal and drainage systems can be a dangerous source of bacteria and should be installed by experts and approved by sanitation authorities. Garbage receptacles need to be behind cabinet doors and easily emptied. State codes typically specify numbers of urinals and toilets. Toilet areas should have floor drainage to facilitate frequent and thorough cleaning. Once again, comply with all local sanitation laws, then add your own special precautions, some of which may involve programming decisions. For example, many staff stress the importance of staff and children washing their hands *frequently* in child care centers.

Comfort

A comfortable space contributes to the good health of young children, as well as to their sense of well-being. Excessive heat or cold increases the incidence of illness and makes children irritable.

When renovating a space, it is important to provide adequate fresh air for every room. Rooms should be free from floor-level drafts and overheating. Sufficient lighting is also important. Play rooms need windows fitted with adjustable shades to protect against glare on bright days and to darken the room for naptime. Light fixtures are built into walls and ceilings to provide sufficient light on dark days. Color is also important to the comfort of children. When painting walls and ceilings and when selecting carpet, care should be taken to choose light, not necessarily bright, colors.

Space utilization

Most centers separate infants from toddlers. Often this is mandated by licensing agencies. Licensing regulations that demand a higher staff ratio for infants (4:1) than for toddlers (6:1) often prompt programs to separate the two groups. Nonetheless, smaller centers often mix babies with toddlers and praise the resulting "sense of family."

As discussed in Chapter 6, "Programming for Infants and Toddlers," many centers divide their space into activity areas.

The center in St. Louis is divided into two large areas. Children are organized into three groups: infants (0 to 18 months), with a staff ratio of 1:4; toddlers (18 to 36 months), with a staff ratio of 1:7; and a preschool group (3 and 4 years old), with a staff ratio of 1:9.

Each center must learn to make the best use of the space available to it, but the following suggestions may be adapted to a variety of settings.

An *infant room* (for children 0 to 9 or 12 months) can be equipped with cribs, adult rocking chair, infant swings, walkers, assorted soft and plastic toys, a baby-level-mirror, a diaper changing area and equipment, and extra changing clothes. A separate space should be available, if possible, for sleep and lunches. Having a separate sleeping room facilitates natural sleep cycles.

A *toddler room* should provide open space so that the children can explore and move about. If space is limited, a path can be arranged down one side of the room for toddlers to cruise. The room should have an old sofa and armchair—for staff and adults to sit on sometimes and for toddlers to climb on at other times. Staff members can also create opportunities for exploration by bringing one or two toddlers along while doing errands in the building.

Arrangements of space and equipment can be based on the same principles as that of any classroom: activity areas or centers of interest, with learning materials stored neatly on low open shelves, most of them accessible to the children. If adults organize the room well and demonstrate concern and respect for the materials and toys, toddlers will imitate their behavior and eventually learn to help care for their own environment.

A center should be designed to be safe but also offer appropriate risks. A child cannot reap the rewards of being autonomous when the center space does not encourage autonomy.

CHAPTER TEN
Policies

Center policies are the guidelines set for how a center is to operate. Some policies are developed in response to licensing requirements, school board interests, school administration rules, or other outside demands. Others are devised in the center by staff in response to their goals for mothers and their children.

Generally center policies are established or refined through collaboration between staff and members of the advisory board. Policies, once decided upon, should be approved by the advisory board in formal session. Once established, relevant policies should be written out and discussed in orientation materials supplied to all program participants and staff.

Policies often cover such areas as:
- criteria for eligibility, selection, enrollment, and termination;
- the days and hours of operation;
- school attendance requirements;
- fees;

- health and safety requirements and procedures;
- helping children develop cooperative behavior;
- parental involvement in the center;
- food; and
- transportation.

Eligibility criteria

Eligibility criteria for both parents and children need to be determined according to the considerations already discussed: demand, program scope, and resources. The program should make every effort to seek out and serve the children of all eligible mothers. At the same time, the center should not try to stretch its resources to do half the job for twice as many participants. Some balance must be struck between demand and resources. If demand significantly outstrips resources, then planning should begin immediately to expand the center. Enrollment criteria should be straightforward and nondiscriminatory.

Basic eligibility criteria, used by most centers, are the child's age and certification of the mother's high school enrollment, regular attendance, grade level, and academic performance. If a mother is out of school, the program usually assesses her commitment to educational goals.

As has been discussed in the chapter on design, setting minimum and maximum ages for a child's participation limits or expands the scope of a center's operations. Decisions are based on the number of potential participants and the capacity of the center. Some centers can accept all children of eligible mothers. Others may have to limit enrollment by restricting the age range of the children or the grade level of the mothers. Minimum ages for infants range from six weeks to two months, maximum ages from one and a half to three and a half years.

All centers require that the mother be committed to regular school attendance. Without this stipulation, the rationale for school-based child care is negated. Most centers on school grounds require that the mother attend the high school where the center is located. Transfers are arranged for mothers from other schools. Centers located off school property have more flexibility in this regard, although to be certain that mothers are attending classes requires a more complicated system of monitoring.

Many centers link continuing participation with the mother's academic commitment. Mothers should maintain a passing average or demonstrate an improved average once child care begins.

Participant selection procedures

Of the centers studied, the Murray-Wright Infant-Toddler Child Development Center and the LYFE Program at Bay Ridge High School have the simplest selection procedures. Mothers meet with the coordinator, fill in the forms, and are accepted on a first-come, first-served basis once need is determined. The coordinator ascertains need, which consists of lack of available or affordable child care and the motivation to complete high school. Forms are simplified. Written consent of the student mother's parents is required.

Other centers have slightly more complicated procedures. The Center for Infant Development in Elizabeth puts students on an eligibility waiting list as soon as the student submits a doctor's note certifying pregnancy and listing a delivery date. Applicants are interviewed and priority given to seniors and to those under sixteen, who are required by law to complete school. The Rule High School Preschool/Parenting Learning Center's director interviews applicants, assists with filling out forms, and provides information on program demands and expectations. Applicants are screened according to their need for child care and their commitment to the program. Priority is given to seniors. The Crib Infant Care Center, as part of the expanded PIIP program in St. Louis, requires a home visit by a social worker to determine need. Applicants may be referred to services in the community other than the child care center.

The Polytechnic Child Care Center in Fort Worth uses a screening committee, consisting of the director, the Adolescent Pregnancy Services coordinator, a community representative, and representatives of the advisory board, to select participants. Screening criteria include: school enrollment or re-enrollment, if the mother has dropped out; a commitment to maintain grades and attendance; "good citizenship"; and documented financial or other extenuating need. Seniors are given first preference for placement in the center.

Demand for services in most centers requires the applicant to place her name on a waiting list in order to become eligible for the next vacancy. Waiting lists maintain relative stability of enrollment, although it is preferable that the wait be very short!

Enrollment

Program registration consists mainly of completing and submitting the proper forms. These may include:
- an information and agreement form to be signed by the student/mother, agreeing to participate according to the rules of the center;
- an enrollment form, asking for emergency contacts, and so on;
- a permission form to be signed by the parent or guardian of the student/mother (this may be necessary unless the student is an emancipated minor);
- a medical examination report on the child; and
- a questionnaire on the infant's behavior patterns and special needs.

If the mother or her infant is under a doctor's care or requires medication, further medical releases may be necessary or permission obtained from the physician to administer medicine to children. If the mother is transferring from another school, this paperwork must be included.

All forms become part of the mother's individual permanent record and should be readily available for review by staff members.

School attendance

School attendance by mothers is usually monitored regularly for compliance with center policies: to ensure that children are not being dropped off at the center, while mothers cut classes; or to determine when mothers are in school and children are not. This requires close liaison with the school's central administrative office. Centers usually insist that children may never be left if the mother is absent. If children are absent without excuse while mothers attend, then the circumstances surrounding this are reviewed. In one center, if mothers have three absences within two weeks, they are placed on a "high-risk" list. The center maintains that experience has shown that there is a high probability these students will drop out of school. The parent is then notified, and if the problem continues, counseling is arranged.

At the Center for Infant Development, mothers' attendance is monitored in the following way: attendance is checked in the home room; high school attendance officers produce a computerized attendance/absence list by 9:30 A.M. and send it to the center, where it is checked by center staff; if a mother is absent but has dropped her baby off at the center, she is notified in writing that this is prohibited; if the practice continues, she is denied child care.

Attendance monitoring is important for several other reasons. Attendance figures are used to compute unit-costs of care to evaluate cost-effectiveness and to make budget projections. In addition, attendance figures can reveal trends in center usage that have implications for future planning. Since centers have generally experienced an increased use of services, a small but steady decline in attendance rates over a long period of time could be a warning signal that something in the program is amiss.

Termination

Termination policies vary. The Crib Infant Care Center allows children five consecutive days of absences. Each situation is considered individually to identify the problem and consider solutions. Chronic lateness is also grounds for termination. At the Polytechnic Child Care Center all children are considered "at risk," and every effort is extended to help the mother keep her child enrolled and in attendance. Officially, three unexcused absences is cause for termination. However, if the mother calls on the day the child is absent, the absence is excused. At Rule High School's Preschool/Parenting Learning Center, termination occurs when a child reaches two years old or the student parent graduates from school. Other circumstances resulting in termination include poor attendance, nonpayment, or lack of cooperation between the parent and center staff.

The centers surveyed stressed the importance of making every effort to keep mothers and children enrolled and active. Staff believe termination should be applied as a last resort. The steps leading to termination should be incremental and clearly outlined. Staff are insistent that mothers be given an opportunity to carefully consider the consequences of their actions.

To discourage false starts, the center's policies for retaining and terminating participants should be clarified in the first interview and stressed throughout the selection procedures. Detail the mother's responsibilities and make clear that failure to live up to these responsibilities could be cause for dismissal from the program. Policies regarding parents' responsibilities should be developed to avoid abuse of the center's services.

Days and hours of operation

Center hours and days of operation are set to provide child care when it is most convenient for those who will use it. The center is responsive to user need. If the center serves many mothers who must depend on public transportation, bus and subway schedules should be considered. Often, opening only fifteen minutes earlier will make the difference between an orderly check-in period and a confused rush. Center policy should clarify whether there are after-school services and set rules covering early dismissals.

Opening and closing times must be firmly respected. Centers tend to open thirty to forty-five minutes before classes begin and stay open until thirty minutes after classes have ended. Some centers offer extended time for children of parents in work-study programs or employed part time, although these allowances need to be carefully monitored for their impact on the budget.

Picking up children late is a problem common to most child care centers but seems to be less of a problem with school-based centers, as staff have ways of monitoring the mother's whereabouts. You will have to work with your mothers so they understand why a child should be picked up on time—otherwise staff end up working overtime, and children are upset by waiting.

Some centers follow a policy of increasing deterrence for mothers who break center rules. The first infraction calls for a warning; the next, a penalty; the third, dismissal from the program.

Most programs are closed if school is not in session. If many parents are working part time or enrolled in work-study programs, the center may make special arrangements to care for children on days when the school is closed, but parents must work part of the day.

It is important to list all days when the center will be closed at the beginning of each term, so that parents may plan ahead for alternative care if they need it.

Fees

The decision of whether or not to charge user fees is made in the planning stages. If the decision is yes, then clearly communicated policies regarding parent fees are essential to ensure that payments are fairly distributed and promptly collected. It is important to choose a fee schedule that will not overly tax the parents. Rates may be set as a flat fee for all participants or computed on a sliding-scale basis, according to income. Fees can be collected weekly, biweekly, or monthly. It is important to set deadlines for payments of fees and to have clear-cut procedures that apply if fees are not paid on time. Depending on funding arrangements, late or nonpayment of fees can develop into a serious problem and detract from a center's capability to meet its expenses. The overwhelming advice is to deal with late payment at once and not to let the parent get behind. Says one staff member: "We are careful to set fees low enough that we know the mother can pay them."

Decide who should collect the fees. This is usually someone without teaching responsibilities, such as a bookkeeper or an administrative assistant. Fees should be recorded by one person and again recorded and deposited by a second person, providing a double check on amounts and accounts. Parents may be asked to pay by the first of the month and considered "delinquent" after the tenth, or whatever system appears most convenient to the center. Some centers collect a one-time registration fee of $5 to $25 to cover initial interviews, record-keeping costs, or medical examinations.

Agreement on policy pertaining to fee payment for unexpected closing, due to weather, heating problems, or other emergency, should be reached. One center created unnecessary hard feelings among parents by insisting on fee payment for two days closed because of snow. The parents argued that since they did not receive care, they should not have to pay for it. Center staff maintained that fees were set to cover participation in the program for the term, not on a pay-for-service basis. This disagreement could easily have been avoided by establishing a clear policy before the situation arose.

Health

To provide a healthy environment for children, the center must establish policies and procedures that protect the well-being of all participants. These policies cover immunizations and check-ups, illness, emergency procedures, and suspected child abuse.

State regulations require, and center procedures should also require, proof of immunizations, medical and dental check-ups, and signed authorization forms for dispensing medications in the center before a child may be enrolled. Assistance in acquiring these documents is usually provided through the center's medical referral network. These documents then become a part of the children's permanent files and should be readily accessible to staff members.

In addition, specific policies should be formulated on what constitutes illness, when a child should be kept at home, and when a child should be removed from the center. These policies also include a procedure, developed in conjunction with school administration, for excusing mothers from classes to care for children when they are ill. This often requires a permanent permission release to be signed by the student mother's parents as well. A copy of the mother's class schedule should be kept on file for ready access in case emergencies develop during the day.

Parents have the responsibility to keep children out of the center and to take them for treatment if conditions such as the following occur: strep throat, chicken pox, lice, vomiting or diarrhea, fever or an associated rash, or untreated impetigo. Children are allowed to return to the center when symptoms subside and with proof of treatment. Such absences are then excused.

When symptoms develop while a child is in the center, parents should be released from class to take their children to a medical practitioner if conditions such as these are present: oral temperature of 101 degrees, vomiting, diarrhea, persistent cough, lice, pain, or other symptoms of acute or contagious illness.

Until the parent arrives, the child should be isolated from other children under close and loving supervision. (The child may not understand why he cannot be with the other children.) If a nurse practitioner is available on site, parents accompany their children immediately to the clinic for examination. Results should be reported to the center director when the examination is completed.

Infectious and communicable diseases are an especially difficult problem for centers. Infants and toddlers are especially vulnerable during an onset of flu, stomach viruses, chicken pox, or lice. When an epidemic situation exists, defined by a certain percentage of illness-related absences, then the center may be forced to close for several days. This is an extreme response and should be carefully described in written policy. If the center has an epidemic or a child looks different than usual, children may be examined carefully for signs of such conditions as impetigo, pinworms, and lice at check-in time.

Safety procedures

Policies regarding fires, accident prevention, and emergencies must be carefully considered, clearly written, and well understood. Post the procedures to be used in case of fire or other emergencies requiring rapid evacuation of the building. Regular fire drills should be an integral feature of center policy. The center director, or whoever is in charge when this sort of emergency occurs, should be the last to leave the center after determining that all procedures have been followed and all children and staff are safe.

Policies designed to prevent accidents are adapted to site conditions. In spite of all precautions, however, accidents are likely to occur. For example, choking on food will happen. Staff should be trained in basic first aid and understand when first aid is appropriate and when it is not. Minor accidents, such as bumps and scrapes, can be treated by center staff and a note made in files on the nature of the injury and the treatment administered, even if it is as simple as: scrape on knee, applied antiseptic and band-aid. It is best to inform the mother of all such incidents.

More serious or life-threatening situations require instant reaction and teamwork. Bleeding must be stopped, an ambulance called, the mother contacted, and other children calmed and supervised. Procedures should be thoroughly discussed in staff meetings.

Emergency medical procedures for staff must be absolutely clear and precise:
- ☐ emergency telephone numbers should be listed next to the telephone;
- ☐ staff members should notify the director or head teacher at once in case of emergency;
- ☐ the director or head teacher should notify the parent and school administration;
- ☐ a medical referral should be arranged; and
- ☐ in an acute situation, professional help must be summoned at once.

Serious accidents must be reported and reviewed. In addition to insurance reports, many programs have accident report forms that are filed with the school and the governing body. Reports should describe the circumstances of the incident, staff response, effectiveness of procedure, and outcome. Above all, the report should be used to answer the question: "Could this accident have been prevented?"

If physical or emotional child abuse is suspected, it should be discussed with the parent and reported to the director. Centers suggest that counseling at the center should be tried before invoking "outside" force. In many states, staff with reasonable cause to suspect child abuse are required by law to report incidents to the state child welfare bureau. The director's primary concern should be to halt any further abuse. If abuse continues, steps will have to be taken to intervene in the home, remove the parent from the program, or seek a court decision for the child's protection. If parents feel the center's judgment made about them is wrong, they have the right to appeal to the advisory board.

Helping children to learn cooperative behavior

All responsible child care centers stress matter-of-fact verbal methods of working with children on unwanted behavior. To encourage self-control, respect for others, and cooperative ways of acting staff must demonstrate these ways of behaving themselves.

At no time and in no situation should any form of corporal punishment, such as spanking, hitting, or shaking, be allowed by anyone in the center, staff or parent. No child should be subjected to pain as a means of changing behavior. No child should be denied meals as a means of punishment. No child should be ridiculed, isolated without a staff member, or verbally abused.

The center's philosophy should be reviewed with the parent upon enrollment. Effective techniques to help children develop positive ways to express and cope with their feelings should be modeled and discussed in group sessions as well as individual counseling.

Parents should be encouraged to discuss any of their parenting practices that are in question—their own methods or those of center staff—in a closed session with appropriate staff.

Parental involvement

The hours and rules for parental involvement in the center should be carefully delineated and respected. For example, the center may expect parents, while in the center, to consider themselves responsible to all children in the center, not just their own. The rules a center establishes for parental involvement will depend on how fully parents are integrated into daily operations. The more parents are involved, the more comprehensive rules should be, and the more thorough pre-involvement training must be.

Food

All programs either provide snacks or allow children to bring snacks from home. Some centers restrict the kinds of snacks that children can bring, banning "junk foods" and encouraging fresh fruits and vegetables. While nutrition is the primary consideration in planning center menus, parents should also be allowed input in the planning process. It may be important to incorporate a variety of ethnic foods in the diet that both are nutritious and reflect home eating habits. Food guidelines might be disseminated through a center handbook. The consulting nutritionist might also provide counseling for improving the nutritive value of foods eaten at home, such as using fresh foods, decreasing cooking times, and balancing the food groups. To prevent choking, policies regarding foods not to be given to small children and appropriate bite sizes should be reviewed.

Transportation

Transportation is often a problem for center participants. While mothers are expected to provide their own transportation to school and to the center, programs often arrange for or provide transportation to referral appointments away from the center. Depending on the program's budget, this may consist of acquiring a van or station wagon for center business or providing bus fare or subway tokens. Limited use of private vehicles might be authorized under stated conditions.

If transportation is provided, parents should be notified when transportation will and will not be available. Conditions of use and a code of conduct in vehicles should be spelled out. State licensing requirements often apply strict rules for transporting parents and children in vehicles, and these should be followed. Informal arrangements, such as using the director's car or asking for volunteer drivers, can lead to dangerous situations or problems with insurance. Policy defines authorized vehicles, appoints certified drivers, and specifies the number of passengers permitted and where children sit. Seatbelts are mandatory. The use of special infant and toddler seats is strongly recommended if this is not already required by law.

Operations and policies manuals

Each of the centers that we visited took pains to develop a comprehensive manual for use by parents, outlining center operations and established policies. Manuals discuss program objectives and describe how the program is designed to meet these objectives. Services are described. The roles and responsibilities of parents are clearly stated, along with terms of participation. Conditions leading to termination of participation in the center are detailed. The manual should also discuss payment of fees and penalties, illness policy, and emergency procedures. Manuals offered guidelines for helping young children develop into happy, curious, and cooperative preschoolers. Staff found that such manuals rendered invaluable assistance for the smooth operation of the center, as mothers were better informed about their own responsibilities and to whom they were responsible as a program participant.

These manuals must be *very readable*. Many young mothers have low basic skills. Make your manual as clear, concise, and attractive as possible.

An operations manual is designed for the use of center employees. It encapsulates the procedures by which a center implements policies, outlines administrative structure, and defines staff roles and responsibilities. An operations manual serves to standardize procedures and expectations, thus reducing procedural errors, allowing staff to perform tasks more competently, and reducing the need for constant supervision. Routine activities as well as emergency procedures are described. Policies pertaining to terms of employment—payment, promotion, termination, vacation, sick days, and benefits—should be set down in definitive form to avoid misunderstanding and possible disagreement.

CHAPTER ELEVEN

Funding

The question of funding has been in the background of all previous planning activities. This chapter will discuss how to locate, secure, and maintain funding for the program that you have designed. This will require:
- developing a working budget;
- writing an effective funding proposal;
- finding the funding sources that will most likely support the kind of center that you have designed; and
- adjusting your budget and funding sources after the initial year or two of operations.

A working budget

A budget is a carefully calculated plan of expected program expenses and incomes. Putting one together is a fairly straightforward exercise in predicting the future. Every possible cost, from renovating a space, applying for licenses, teacher salaries and benefits, to the price of diapers, needs to be considered and closely approximated. Otherwise, start-up funds may prove inadequate and cripple the program from its inception. As well, several budget-related decisions need to be made that will shape the program, such as, should mothers be charged a fee for using child care, and if so, how large should it be?

Those who have experience with other types of programs will already have a basic understanding of how budgeting works. Others may view it, probably correctly, as an imposing task. It is imposing because of the sheer volume of details that must be considered, but the framework has already been assembled. What remains is to fill in the spaces with applied imagination and common sense.

Calculating expenses

Quality child care is not inexpensive, but the costs to community and family will be even greater in years to come if children are neglected or mothers forced to terminate their education. Providing child care to young mothers now will prove more economical for the future. If this conviction is supported by community policymakers, then adequate financing can usually be found. Funding sources, however, like to know that their money is being well spent and demand a detailed account of expenses. So far, planning has been concerned with the more theoretical questions of design; now it must be decided how much it will cost to implement the program components that have been selected. Build on previous work, make a list of day-to-day program priorities, and answer the following essential questions:

Who is the program for? When will it begin? How many children? What ages? What are the operating days and hours? Will some children attend part time—say during school hours but not in the after-school program run from 3 to 6 P.M.?

Which activities are essential to the program's daily operations? What is needed in terms of space, equipment, supplies, and personnel to provide these activities?

Where will the program be housed? Will the space be purchased, rented, or donated? What are the costs for maintenance, utilities, and upkeep?

How will meals and snacks be provided? What are the costs of food and facilities?

What donated goods and services does the program expect to obtain?

What are staffing requirements? Required teacher/infant and teacher/toddler ratios? Expected education and salary levels? Does the program require other on-site specialists, such as a nurse or counselor? Will volunteers be used? How many paid training days will be required for staff members? What benefits will be offered to them?

Translating answers into dollar amounts will probably require many drafts before planners are satisfied that the budget will work. In a very real sense, budget decisions are policy decisions. They should be shared and deliberated.

It is crucial to distinguish between operating expenses, which are costs for normal daily operations, and start-up expenses, which will include many one-time-only costs and purchases. The space will almost certainly need to be renovated to meet state and local standards. Cribs, tables, chairs, playground equipment, desks, a typewriter, pots and pans, a telephone—all necessary educational, administrative, and service purchases that will make it possible for the program to open its doors should be included in the start-up budget. It may be helpful at this point to examine budgets from other child care centers or from similar programs.

Budgeting categories are considered in detail below.

Expenses

Personnel

Because child care is labor intensive, personnel costs are typically the largest budget expense, ranging from 70 to 85 percent of operating costs. The temptation to skimp on salaries and benefits should be resisted as this most often proves counterproductive. The quality of personnel will make or break a program. Therefore, it is in the program's best interest to offer competitive wages and benefits. Incentive raises should be built in to encourage and keep good personnel. Underpaid staff tend to be less dedicated and turn over frequently, which translates into a reduction in the center's quality of care and an increase in administrative tasks and, therefore, time.

Staff benefits include employment insurance, Worker's Compensation, and FICA, which are required by law, and such benefits as health insurance, paid vacation, sick leave, in-service days, or contribution to a retirement fund, which may be optional. A program administered through the school district will need to conform to established salary and benefit policies. Group employee health insurance can be arranged through a private insurer, or the program may be included under a school's policy. Employer and employees typically split the cost of health coverage in a group plan. Allowing staff to accrue one day of paid vacation and one day of unpaid sick leave for every month they work, up to a reasonable limit, is common policy and provides a further incentive for them to stay with the program. While individual circumstances vary, a common custom is to allow 16 to 25 percent of total salaries to cover benefits.

The program director will be the highest-paid employee. In the centers visited, yearly salaries ranged from $12,500 to $30,000. Substitute teaching flexibility can be built in by reducing the work week for all teachers and keeping an extra person on the payroll. Teachers are hired with the understanding that they will be expected to fill in during emergencies. This adds to benefit expenses but reduces the likelihood of being understaffed due to unexpected teacher absences. Otherwise, the director often functions as substitute-in-residence.

Space and utilities

Most spaces that were not originally designed for child care need to be renovated to meet licensing requirements. Money must be allotted for kitchen and bathroom facilities, protection for windows and stairways, fencing around the play yard, new floor covering, and architect or designer's fees. Estimates for space alterations can be obtained, usually at no cost, from local contractors. The best approach is to set up in a donated space in the school itself, where classrooms comprise an in-kind contribution to the program. Otherwise, rent will have to be estimated.

Utilities—heat, light, gas, water, and telephone—can be expensive. If you have located a space, the utility companies can usually tell you what the previous tenant paid, but keep in mind that they were probably not caring for infants. Utilities are also a common in-kind contribution to child care centers by schools and other sponsoring agencies.

Equipment and furniture

The budget must also include the costs of standard office equipment (such as filing cabinets, a desk, typewriter, computer) and its upkeep. Estimates for administrative equipment will be provided by local office furniture stores. The center will also need educational and child care equipment, such as playground equipment, cribs, tables and chairs, scales, and so forth. Estimates on the cost of educational supplies can be obtained from educational equipment companies.

Food service equipment should also be considered and a decision made whether the center should have a complete and self-contained kitchen or make do with a refrigerator and hot plate. This decision will hinge on the size and layout of the selected space and arrangements with the school if the center is on-site.

Supplies

Costs for administration/office supplies for keeping records, correspondence, printing, postage, and such must be estimated. Costs for supplies used by and for children should be calculated. This category will include books, paper, art supplies, toys, and entertainment for older children and the various items involved in infant care: diapers or diaper service, laundry, bottles, teethers, and such.

Costs for food supplies—meals, snacks, and formula—must also be studied. A decision should be made on the extent to which the center will store, prepare, and serve its own meals. Often arrangements can be made to use the school cafeteria for lunch, and center facilities can be used to serve morning and afternoon snacks. USDA child care feeding program guidelines can be used to estimate the kinds, amounts, and costs of foods that will need to be offered.

Publicity/Recruitment expenses

Every budget will need some money set aside to provide publicity for the center's activities, to advertise its existence, and to recruit participants. This will typically consist of printing costs for pamphlets, flyers, center policies handbooks, and employee manuals.

Insurance

Insurance is essential to the responsible operation of a child care center and should be included in administrative costs. Most funding agencies require proof of insurance, and schools will demand it. Generally, insurance should include coverage for fire and theft, worker's compensation for staff, and public liability for children, parents, and visitors on the center's premises. Other forms of insurance may be advisable, depending on the circumstances. Consult an insurance agent for the appropriate package and estimated costs or explore inclusion under the school district's coverage.

Overhead

Funding agencies will demand proper bookkeeping and expect a yearly audit to be performed by an outside source. The services of a bookkeeper may be obtained on a monthly or bimonthly basis to monitor expenses and compute the payroll, depending on funding arrangements. Often the center's fiscal agent can handle these details as an in-kind contribution. A "cushion" may be built in to cover unexpected expenses.

Sources of income

Income may consist of program-generated monies (mainly user fees), in-kind service contributions, and outside grants and donations.

User fees

After estimating expenses, a decision should be made regarding the portion that can be realistically covered by user fees. Most school-based centers are targeted to low-income mothers, who are on public assistance or depend on their families or a new husband for support. Mothers who receive child support or other aid could be asked to contribute a portion for care and feeding of their infants.

A center without outside funding of any sort would have to collect the actual cost of operations from parents. In most cases this would make services inaccessible to adolescent mothers. Many centers, however, feel that minimal fees are important for several reasons. Fees may make up part of the matching funds that some government grants require. Fees serve to stretch outside monies, allowing the program to make other necessary purchases or expand services into other areas. Moreover, many center planners feel that when parents share in the cost of child care, they have a heightened sense of involvement in the center's operations and gain a more realistic sense of the costs of raising children. Paying child care fees becomes a part of their parental responsibility.

There are several ways to set fees, as a flat rate, sliding scale, or subsidy. Flat fees should be set low enough so that all mothers who need child care can afford it. This approach minimizes the income potential for the center, however.

As an alternative, many centers use a sliding scale. Fees are graduated from no payment for mothers, or for the mother's parents, when their income falls below the established poverty line, to full payment for the rare mother who could afford the full cost of care for her child. The sliding scale considers the individual family situation, its net income, medical and other essential expenses, and number of family members, and it may be adjusted if these factors change.

Subsidies for eligible participants through Title XX funds can provide considerable income.

Fee income is not always as dependable as one would like to think. Especially in the first year, enrollment may fall below target levels. Children may be withdrawn or mothers transferred out of the school, leaving an empty slot that may take weeks to fill. With a sliding scale, mothers' incomes might vary significantly from year to year, leaving a deficit that must be made up some other way. Since operating expenses vary little whether or not an individual child is present on a given day, there is little reason to reduce or waive fees for absences. Many centers feel that the regular fee should be assessed in order to hold the child's place in the program.

Once again, decisions to charge fees and the form these fees will take are policy decisions that will affect recruitment and enrollment practices. In simplified economic terms, lower rates tend to broaden the enrollment base, while higher rates tend to restrict it. Much will depend on the envisioned size and scope of the center and the characteristics of the target population.

In-kind contributions

Contributions in the form of rent, utilities, supplies, and labor should be given a monetary value and included when computing costs and income. Often foundations and some government entitlements will require the program to match their grants with a stated level of in-kind monies. It is also important to include these hidden costs and incomes to have a realistic assessment of the total cost of the program. Arrangements may change unexpectedly, and the center forced to bear the expenses itself or find another donor.

In-kind services play a crucial role in the budgets of all of the centers visited, although the mix of services and amounts varies. Space and utilities are a common donation and relieve the center of serious financial burdens. However, by accepting in-kind contributions, the center typically surrenders some measure of its control and autonomy. These trade-offs should be carefully weighed.

Budget approval

The completed budget should be approved by the advisory board or other sponsoring agency. What is left when program-generated monies and in-kind goods and services are subtracted from estimated yearly expenses is what you will need to generate from other funding sources.

The funding proposal

Funding proposals of various centers are similar in structure and in purpose. They are meant to convince a funding agency that the need for a service is real and immediate, that the program design will address and alleviate the need, that the planners are capable of administering the program, and that money will be properly apportioned and well spent. The proposal is a synopsis of planning efforts and may be as short as two pages or as long as twenty.

Statement of need

The proposal opens with a statement of need, which should present the results of the community needs assessment and any other evidence that is relevant. Present the facts clearly and concisely. They should support the program's argument for providing services yet not bog down in too much detail. Define the target population in terms of characteristics and numbers. If a site has been tentatively selected, concentrate on the specific numbers and needs of potential participants.

Objectives

The program's objectives should be listed and described as they were decided by the planning committee. The objectives should encompass the scope of the center and should be amenable to measurable outcomes. Which particular needs will each objective address? What are the outcomes expected from these objectives?

Program activities

How have program activities been designed to achieve each of the center's objectives? The theoretical or proven basis for the usefulness of these activities should be discussed briefly. Discuss the origin of the center's model of services. Describe the center's program for infants, for toddlers, for mothers, fathers, or other students, and show how these are compatible with program objectives.

Staffing and management

How will the program be managed? What are staffing levels? What are roles and job responsibilities? Discuss the capabilities of key staff or hiring criteria. Provide a timetable of start-up operations.

Budget

How will funds be administered? Provide a budget, detailing expenditures in set categories, including estimated center-generated funds, in-kind contributions, and additional requested funds. Separate start-up from operating expenses. Offer explanations or justifications for line items that appear particularly high or low.

The funding proposal should be approved by the advisory board, the proposed umbrella agency or fiscal agent, and often by the board of education, as well. Although, in some cases, money has been appropriated before approval and used to convince the school board to go along, it would seem best to gain all the necessary assurances before the proposal is submitted to a funding source. This strengthens the proposal's appeal and may avoid conflicts at a later date.

Sample outline of initial funding proposal

I. Organizational information
   A. School system and superintendent
   B. School and principal
   C. Contact person
   D. Title and date of proposal

II. Brief summary

III. Statement of need
   A. Problem to be addressed
   B. Background to proposed program
   C. Overview of school system involvement and major accomplishments in the area

IV. Objectives

V. Plan of operations
   A. Program activities
   B. Staffing and management
   C. Documentation/Evaluation

VI. Budget
   A. Project budget
   B. Support requested from funding source
   C. Other committed resources
   D. Plan for future funding

Securing funding

Funding sources

Funding sources varied greatly across the six centers that were studied and often depended on the initiative of sponsoring agencies and individuals. All of the centers agreed, however, that the center should not depend too heavily on a single source. Using several funding sources guards against government cutbacks or cuts in school budgets. Some sources are more interested in providing start-up funding, while others prefer to support a program that is already operating.

Our centers solicited and received funding from a variety of sources, including:
- local boards of education;
- local community development programs and initiatives;
- special grants from local public agencies supportive of the program;
- private foundations;
- social services block grants;
- state offices of education; and
- Title XX child care subsidies for parents who receive AFDC.

It is important to establish a dialogue with potential funding sources early in the support/resources/design process. Find out what their interests are, what programs they have funded before, and their funding criteria.

Federal and state grants that should be researched include Title XX, the Federal Educational Consolidation Improvement Act, Vocational Education Grants, and grants offered by state departments of education and departments of health and human services. Government money is often linked to attendance or may require the center to put up matching funds from other sources.

City governments may also be a source of support by providing community development funds or other types of grants.

Many foundations have shown a great interest in supporting efforts to provide school-based child care services. Foundations based in the community were particularly disposed toward funding a local center, as shown by centers in St. Louis, Knoxville, and Fort Worth. These foundations should be contacted through the grants office by telephone first to determine their interests or previous efforts in this area. They may allocate monies once a year or continuously throughout the year.

In many communities, privately financed agencies hold an annual fundraising campaign together. The goal of such a campaign depends on the collective needs of member agencies. Funds are allocated to participating agencies in proportion to approved budget requests and to the success of the campaign. A child care center that is incorporated, not-for-profit, and meets specific standards may be able to share in jointly raised funds. Use of the money is normally restricted to making up shortfalls in operating expenses, rather than for start-up or expansion.

Centers have also successfully solicited funds from corporations and businesses located in the community.

Funding sources, particularly government grants, are continually shifting and making changes in eligibility criteria and targeted programs. Those persons who administer grant programs are extremely knowledgeable and can offer up-to-date advice and suggestions.

Funding strategies

Although most school systems make at least in-kind contributions to the centers, only the LYFE center at Bay Ridge High School is completely financed by the Board of

Education, New York City. Carol Burt-Beck was brought on to the central office staff of the school system to develop a program for the school system. Although start-up funding came, in part, from a citywide initiative on adolescent pregnancy, it was assumed that the Board of Education would provide full support in the future. The center's objective of keeping adolescent mothers in school matched perfectly with the school system's goal of reducing dropout, for which monies had been set aside. While integrating a child care center into the school system's budget virtually ensures its permanence, most centers will not have such direct access in the beginning.

A number of centers grew out of or were sponsored by existing programs, which provided or assisted with start-up funding. The center at Vashon High School in St. Louis was an expansion of a well-established program for teen parents, which was supported by private foundations and the school system. Start-up funding was provided by the local Danforth Foundation, with approval from the superintendent and the school board. Funds are administered by the school system and directed through Vashon High School's principal. The program also receives matching state funds from the State Office of Education, Desegregation Division.

In Elizabeth, New Jersey, the Center for Infant Development was initiated by a school social worker who wrote a proposal to the New Jersey Department of Human Services for Title XX funds. These funds represent the most significant portion of the center's budget, since most program participants are considered disadvantaged. Community development funds were secured to purchase and renovate the center's present site. In-kind contributions are supplied by city health and human services agencies and by the school district. Moreover, the United Way, local foundations, businesses, and private donors have made up expenses that government monies and in-kind contributions did not cover. Funds are administered through the school district's director of Community Services, Federal and State Programs, who has fairly tight control over expenditures.

Start-up funds for the child care center at Polytechnic High School, Fort Worth, were solicited by proposals written by the YWCA, the program's umbrella agency. Major funders were the City of Fort Worth, through a community development block grant, the locally based McFarland Day Nursery Fund, and the Fort Worth Independent School District, which renovated the space, paid some staff salaries, and contributed in-kind services. The director explained that the center was begun as a pilot program, operating on city and foundation monies. If it proves successful in meeting its goals, it is likely that the center will be institutionalized, at least partially, by inclusion in the school district's budget.

Initial funding for The Preschool/Parenting Learning Center of Rule High School, Knoxville, came from a state-administered grant under the Federal Educational Consolidation Improvement Act, Chapter II, solicited by proposal, and from the Levi Strauss Foundation, which contacted the center's director. Operating funds come mainly from these two sources, with a small portion from user fees and private donations. The center is administered through the city's Alternative Learning Center, but the school system acts as its fiscal agent. The center director makes purchase order requests through the high school principal.

A number of recommendations can be based on these examples. Networking has been shown, once again, to be a successful approach to locating funding. It is important to contact people who are familiar with government and private funding sources, such as personnel in grants and funding departments of the school system or local colleges. A knowledgeable source will save time and help you avoid dead ends. Strong educational components allowed centers to tap educational grants from social service agencies or from the federal government. Laboratory centers received vocational education monies. If mothers met low-income or disadvantaged criteria, subsidies were available through Title XX so long as these funds were administered by an acceptable agency. Funding success depended greatly on program components, so it is important to go back over the center's design to match components with potential sources.

Budgeting for the future

A center's funding cycle will typically go through three phases: seed, maintenance, and expansion. The first budget will include start-up, or seed, monies, as well as operating expenses for the opening year. In most cases, these funds will come from outside sources and be specifically earmarked for establishing a pilot or model program. If implementation proves successful, the following year will concentrate on maintaining the activities of the center at established levels. Many foundations offer one- or two-year grants and will expect the center to locate more permanent sources of funding beginning in the second year. This usually means relying more heavily on user fees, in-kind contributions, and community, state, or federal monies.

The ultimate goal for many centers will be integration into the school district's budget. This will require proving yourself and establishing an effective evaluation process that can measure program outcomes. It also requires effective lobbying within the school and community for a permanent status. Implementation is a test of the program and its components. Staffing levels may prove inadequate, expenses higher than anticipated, and demand overwhelming. At this point, the program may wish to expand to more fully do its job, which may require rethinking and redesigning. Participant outcomes and implementation results may then be used to attract further one-time grants or to justify a larger share of appropriated funds. So long as demand for the program's services is high and community needs remain, there is adequate reason to seek out funds for expansion.

Budget analysis

After implementation has begun, every program will want to analyze its budget projections in terms of operations realities. To accomplish this, administrators, or a committee appointed by the governing body, will want to answer the following questions:

> Have operating expenses been estimated correctly? Have all overhead costs been included and equally distributed among program components? Seemingly inconsequential costs can mount up over the course of the year.

> Do actual costs differ radically from projected costs? If so, which budget categories need to be revised? Were start-up costs higher or lower than expected? Did cash flow problems develop?

> What are the costs of care per child? What are the costs of services per mother? How do these figures compare with state and national averages?

> Is every projected service needed to meet the program's stated objectives? Have results justified expenditures or could money be better used elsewhere?

> Do service areas overlap? Is there duplication of effort that can be eliminated?

> Do higher expenses reflect actual need and effective usage or waste and inefficiency?

Only after the oversight committee has closely scrutinized each budget item should it consider expanding the budget or cutting back services. Sometimes surpluses exist in certain categories that can be reallocated to others.

No matter how thorough planners are, creating a balanced budget is usually a matter of trial and error. Each financial statement must be used to adjust future projections.

CHAPTER TWELVE

Management and Evaluation

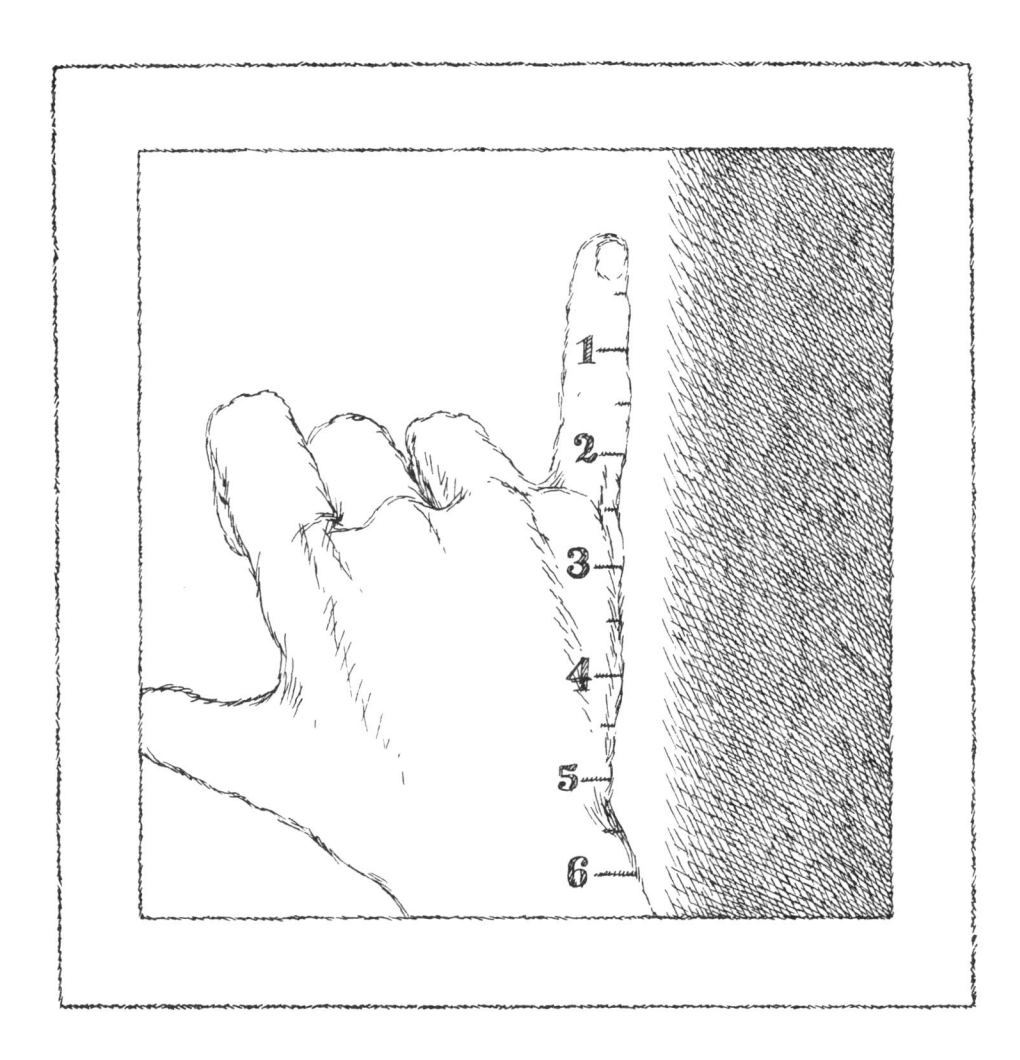

Every program needs a director with a strong administrative background. Administrative responsibilities include staff leadership and supervision; monitoring program operations; liaison with the advisory board, school administration, and other agencies; and the issues to be covered in this chapter—financial management, records management, and evaluation.

Financial management

Good financial management should complement sound center policies. The elements of good financial management include:

Responsibility. Formal systems for recording funds received and disbursed are set up and followed. Checks and balances are built in. Income and expenses are recorded in more than one place. People check one another. Tasks are broken down into manageable pieces, and each piece assigned to an appropriate individual within the program. Lines of responsibility are clearly drawn. Detailed records document all financial activities.

Clarity. Procedures are clear and simple. Everyone in the program knows where to go for what, when, and how. Ordering and purchasing procedures are clearly defined. Written forms are designed so that information is easy to understand.

Foresight. As much as possible, contingencies are considered, alternatives discussed, and funds set aside as a cushion against financial emergencies. Cash-flow problems are anticipated and avoided.

Every program requires a workable bookkeeping system that allows administrators to keep track of the funds flowing in and out. Most centers employ a professional accountant on a part-time basis to handle payroll and to keep the books balanced. Cash-basis accounting is the simplest system to use. However, an accountant should be consulted to design a system that is right for you.

Ordering materials and services for the program may be handled by one person, usually the director, or by several persons, each responsible for a particular area of the program. One staff member may be responsible for food and sanitation supplies, another for educational materials, and a third for office supplies. Orders are based on allocations for each category of the budget. Whatever method is adopted, the system should define who is permitted to order; who must grant approval; how ordering is to be done; how purchases are to be recorded; what method of payment is to be used.

Regardless of who orders materials and services, one person should have sole responsibility for writing the checks. This way, he or she can establish a uniform system of making and recording payments. Payments are recorded in a number of places to guard against loss of an entry. Computer files should be backed up with a written system. Some centers use a dual-signature checking account, which requires the signature of two individuals before a payment is validated. Although occasionally it may be inconvenient for two people to see and sign a check, this procedure builds in a further check and balance to encourage fiscal responsibility.

Money coming in, like money going out, should be recorded in multiple locations. Parents' fees comprise the bulk of incoming cash. These payments should be accepted by one individual who records the name, date, and amount of payment before passing it on to the bookkeeper, who then records the payments, makes a credit against the remitter's name, and then deposits the money. All cash received is deposited daily in the center's account. Cash should never be left lying around as an unnecessary temptation. Incoming cash should not be used for petty cash purchases. The system you adopt should record the amount of money received on a given day and keep track of total payments received from different individuals and funding sources.

Cash-flow problems are common in child care. When a program has income from federal, state, or local governments, monies may be received only after service has been delivered. Because reimbursement procedures are complex, there may be a lag between when money is paid out and when funds are received. Similarly, when parents fall behind in paying user fees, centers can fall short of funds at the end of the month. Programs that spend large sums of money at once, rather than in incremental amounts, also tend to have cash-flow problems. While some situations may be unavoidable and will need to be covered by a bank loan, others can be avoided by doing a cash-flow analysis.

The goal of a cash-flow analysis is to match the timing of cash inflow with cash

outflow. Do as much as possible to speed up the cash coming in and to slow down the cash going out. This requires:
- identifying cash inflows;
- identifying cash outflows;
- summarizing both by month;
- subtracting monthly expenditures from incomes as they are currently scheduled and examining the cumulative results; and
- rescheduling incoming payments to precede out-going expenses to establish a positive cash-flow pattern.

The purpose of cash-flow analysis is to avoid running the program with a crisis mentality, that is, constantly running to the board needing money to make routine operational expenses. Crisis budgeting is a result of poor foresight and planning. Often, solving a cash-flow problem is as simple as ordering smaller amounts of materials and supplies more frequently. Purchase of consumables is easier to adjust than payroll, which usually remains fairly constant month after month. Cutting wages and postponing paychecks are unacceptable ways of dealing with a shortage of funds.

Records management

Keeping careful records of center activities serves many essential purposes. First, records may be used to further document the needs of participants in order to assess program priorities, to justify funding requests, and to formulate plans for expansion. Records of expenditures assist planning and budgetary oversight and should be submitted to governing bodies and funding agencies to demonstrate responsible fiscal management. Parents' files are used to track rates of participation and to monitor compliance with center policies. Children's files are used to record problems, to monitor progress, and to document the success of interventions. Staff files are used to compile payroll, compute benefits, and evaluate performance. In short, records are used to supervise and evaluate every aspect of program operations.

Such administrative tasks as compiling enrollment lists, checking attendance, completing reports for governing bodies, checking the payroll, keeping referral records, or planning the weekly menu can require full-time effort on the part of the director. This burden can be shifted somewhat to teachers, staff, and other administrative volunteers, but the director retains full oversight responsibility. Center administrators and staff will likely devise their own system of recording and filing, based on experience and necessity. However, the simpler the system, the easier it will be to maintain. Standard forms make it easier for the director and staff to fill in the blanks with needed information.

The collection, storage, and retrieval of information within a program can be complex. In large programs it can become a specialty in and of itself. What follows are a few suggestions to make the process more orderly, less costly, and easier to manage.

Records management begins when information is recorded, and responsibilities for recording data should be allocated through staff job descriptions. Initially, information categories should be linked to the purposes of program development, budgetary oversight, and program evaluation. Additional categories may be added as need is recognized and time becomes available.

Develop standard forms to cover each purpose and file them in a standardized manner to allow consistent access. Information categories should be carefully defined and reviewed with staff to ensure that information is collected and recorded in a consistent and comparable manner. The filing system is organized according to category and purpose, using headings that are clearly understood. Ambiguity leads to unnecessary multiple filing or to misplaced information.

Reducing the complexity of recording and filing information reduces the costs in payroll and time of record management. Simplify! Follow these suggestions:

- reduce narrative descriptions to summarizing observations and interviews;
- use summary sheets, checklists, and other similar forms whenever possible;
- use handwritten entries whenever possible to reduce typing and reproduction costs; and
- study the relative costs of photocopying and computerized recording and filing. The center may explore access to school facilities for these ends.

No matter what method is used, storing unnecessary and outdated records is a waste of space and money. Records are reviewed periodically to determine which should remain active, which should be moved to inactive status, and which should be discarded. Information linked to child and parent outcomes is periodically shifted to a permanent database to be used for evaluation purposes.

Extraneous or outdated records are discarded after applicable statutes of limitations have passed. Fiscal information, once it is recorded in the center's books, provides the permanent and official record of financial operations. Invoices, cancelled checks, timesheets, and similar documents should be kept no longer than is required by law. Certain memoranda of meetings or announcements, for example, may be discarded, but memoranda regarding policy changes or personnel problems should be retained. Important directives should be included in center handbooks, manuals, and lists of rules. Policies should be established regarding how long family records are to be retained after participants are no longer enrolled and which information should pass into the center's permanent database. In general, all records, other than official documents, are discarded as soon as their usefulness for current operations is finished or as soon as they can be legally discarded. Essential outcome data is summarized and filed separately.

Personnel

Employee files include the résumé and application for employment, notes from employment interviews, home and emergency telephone numbers, information on salary and benefits, medical records, records of any problems with the employee, and copies of performance evaluations, if they are used.

Evaluation

Evaluation is an ongoing program concern. Although center staff are always looking critically at their own performance, formal evaluation mechanisms allow the director to demonstrate the program's progress in meeting established goals and objectives in terms of measurable outcomes. A formal evaluation should be designed to:

- provide administrators with documentation of program implementation and operations;
- assess the outcomes of program components through analysis of participant records or survey data; and
- function as part of a consistent information feedback process that allows administrators and project staff to measure progress and plan for future development.

Evaluation of a child care program designed to serve adolescent mothers requires looking at parenting and student outcomes, as well as child care outcomes. Both purposes require establishing a permanent database that records information for incoming participants, a means for assessing performance levels according to objective criteria, and a method for comparing pre- and post-program levels.

Child care outcomes

Incoming data collected for children should include: age, gender, race/ethnicity, language spoken in the home, size and weight, and relative age/development performance according to a standardized assessment scale. Periodic assessments will have to be administered to check a child's progress. As norms for each developmental stage are fairly clearly defined, individualized plans can be used to establish goals for children. Then the staff can use a variety of methods to measure attainment of these goals. Rates of improvement can be documented and capabilities can be compared with standard averages. Thus administrators can determine a success rate for their interventions.

Individual child care objectives should be translated into outcomes that can be measured. For example, a center objective is to encourage daily contact between infants and mothers. The mother's attendance in the center should be recorded and overall attendance rates computed to demonstrate that interactions are, indeed, taking place. While this may seem elementary, many centers keep attendance records for children but none for parents and are thus unable to monitor parental participation in the center. Another center objective may be to ensure appropriate nutrition. Children would be expected to improve in size, weight, and health due to balanced diet, each of which can be measured. While it is more difficult to put a numerical value on health, administrators can compare sick days in the first term with the number of sick days in later terms of program participation and rely on the assessment of medical practitioners. Practitioners can be asked to rate the relative health of each child at the time of enrollment and during all subsequent examinations. As has been suggested, a child development specialist can link learning objectives with social, physical, and developmental outcomes. How does the child compare with others the same age in acquiring social skills? How does the child compare in acquiring motor skills? Is improvement evident, and can it be described and documented? Such are the challenges of designing an effective and convincing evaluation process.

Student parent outcomes

The principal goal of all child care centers targeted for adolescent mothers is to assist the completion of their education. Expected outcomes for participating mothers would be improved absenteeism and tardiness rates, improved academic performance, a positive outlook toward school completion, and an increased rate of graduation for program participants compared to nonparticipants.

Measuring improvement in these areas requires collecting data for participants before and after enrollment in the program and gaining access to comparative information collected by the school system.

The following information should be solicited from mothers as a routine part of enrollment procedures: age, race/ethnicity, marital status, first language, number of children, living arrangements, grade level, and attitude toward graduation. The school office should supply a record of absenteeism and tardiness, grade point average, standardized test scores, credits acquired, and any disciplinary actions. This information should become part of the center's permanent database. Care should be taken to ensure that personal information is accessible only to appropriate staff and that participants' privacy is respected.

For purposes of comparison, data should be compiled about program attendance and participation, persistence in the program, completion of the program or reasons for termination, and, again, school office data after enrollment in the program. Improvement in attendance and academic performance after enrollment may be attributed to the success of program interventions. The number of graduates is the ultimate indicator. Program staff can keep track of rates of graduation for program participants and compare this with the rate of the student body as a whole, with the rate of all female students, or with the rate of a group of mothers who are not being helped in such an intensive way. However, many school systems do not record reasons for dropping out, nor do they have any clear idea of how many students are pregnant or even have children. Therefore, providing a clear-cut control group is difficult or impossible.

This is a problem inherent in many school recordkeeping systems and inhibits a truly scientific center evaluation. Many pregnant and parenting adolescents simply "fall through the cracks" and are lumped together with other "problem" students. Center staff often proved instrumental in pushing the high school to develop more stringent recording methods.

Establishing an internal evaluation methodology, as outlined above, is an important and often neglected program consideration. Administrators should also consider a periodic external evaluation. This requires hiring a private, objective evaluator to interview staff and participants, to collect new data and review compiled information, and to report on improving center activities. Often the school system is willing to pay for such an evaluation to justify the costs of the program or to examine the model of services as a prelude for expansion into other sites.

Summary

Successful program operations is a result of combining policies, management skills, and an evaluation process that funnels important information back to program administrators. Information feedback is indispensable and is built on effective communications between participants and staff, between staff and the director, and between the director and the advisory board or school administrators. Parents, staff, director, and the advisory board should discuss the effect of center policies and be open to change. Each party should have channels through which to request and effect change. Assessment leads to reassessment in an unbroken loop. In this way, the program develops and grows as an organic entity, responsive to the needs and wishes of participants, responsible to those who support it, and efficient in the allocation and use of public resources.

* * *

While not pretending to be the definitive authority and guide to school-based child care, this guide exists to provide encouragement and support for those in schools who have recognized the needs of adolescent parents and seek to provide solutions. The suggestions offered in these pages should be taken as advice and improved on through experience. Each of the centers included here strives to provide services in its own way, according to situation and circumstances. One thing can be said of them all: They have taken a thousand details and combined them into a program that both participants and staff can call their own. They have combined the goals of helping young mothers complete school and become successful parents with the goal of providing a healthy, stimulating environment for the infants and children of teen mothers. In the process they are positively transforming what we can expect of school. They are keeping young mothers and their babies in school together in an effort to improve the lives of both young persons and to avoid the tragedies of childhood deprivation and continued poverty. They invite you to devise a plan that will work for your community and for those who need it the most—the young mothers and children, who want the chance to make it in the world.

CHAPTER THIRTEEN

Additional Resources for Program Planning

I. Books and articles

Serving teenage parents

Ascher, Carol. *Improving Schooling to Reduce Teenage Pregnancy.* No. 28 of *ERIC Digests.* New York: ERIC/Clearinghouse on Urban Education, December 1985.

Ascher, Carol. *Pregnant and Parenting Teens: Statistics, Characteristics and School-Based Support Services.* No. 1 in *Trends and Issues* series. New York: ERIC/Clearinghouse on Urban Education, No. 1, April 1985, p. 1.

Baldwin, Wendy and Virginia Cain. "The Children of Teenage Parents," in *Teenage Sexuality, Pregnancy and Childbearing,* Frank Furstenberg, Richard Lincoln, and Jane Menken, eds. Philadelphia: University of Pennsylvania Press, 1981.

Card, Josefina and Lauress Wise. "Teenage Mothers and Teenage Fathers: The Impact of Early Childbearing on the Parents' Personal and Professional Lives," in *Family Planning Perspectives,* 10, 1978.

Children's Defense Fund. See Periodicals section for *Adolescent Pregnancy Prevention Clearinghouse Papers*.

Chilman, Catherine S., ed. *Adolescent Pregnancy and Childbearing: Findings from Research*, U.S. Department of Health and Human Services, NIH Publication #81-2077, December 1980.

Dunkle, Margaret C. and Bernice Sandler. *Sex Discrimination Against Students: Implications of the Educational Amendments of 1972*. Washington, DC: Association of American Colleges, November 1975.

Dunkle, Margaret C. *Adolescent Pregnancy and Parenting: Evaluating School Policies and Programs from a Sex Equity Perspective*. Washington, DC: Council of Chief State School Officers, Resource Center on Educational Equity, 1985.

Foster, Susan. *Preventing Teenage Pregnancy: A Public Policy Guide*. Washington, DC: Council of State Policy and Planning Agencies, 1986.

Frank, Daniel. *Deep Blue Funk and Other Stories: Portraits of Teenage Parents*. Chicago: Ounce of Prevention Fund, University of Chicago Press, 1983.

Furstenberg, Frank, J. Brooks Gunn, and S. Philip Morgan. *Adolescent Mothers in Later Life*. New York: Cambridge University Press, 1987.

Grow, Lucille J. *Early Childrearing by Young Mothers: A Research Study*. Washington, DC: Child Welfare League of America, 1979.

Haggstron, Gus et al. *Teenage Parents: Their Ambitions and Attainments*. Santa Monica, CA: Rand Corporation, 1981.

Klerman, Lorraine. "Evaluating Service Programs for School-Age Parents: Design Problems," in *Evaluation and the Health Professionals*, Vol. 1, No. 5, Sage Publications, Inc., March 1979, pp. 55–70.

Klerman, L. V. and J. Jekel. *School-Age Mothers: Problems, Programs and Policy*. Hamden, CT: Shoe String Press, 1973.

Life Planning Education: A Youth Development Program. Washington, DC: Center for Population Options, 1985.

McCarthy, James and Ellen S. Radish. "Education and Childbearing Among Teenagers," in *Family Planning Perspectives*, 14:3, May/June 1982.

McGee, Elizabeth. *Too Little, Too Late: Services for Teenage Parents*. A Report to the Ford Foundation, October 1982. New York: Available from the Ford Foundation, Office of Reports.

McGee, Elizabeth. *Training for Transition: A Guide for Helping Young Mothers Develop Employability Skills*. New York: Manpower Demonstration Research Corporation, 1985.

Miller, Shelby. *Children as Parents: Final Report on a Study of Childbearing and Childrearing Among 12–15-Year Olds*. Edison, NJ: Child Welfare League of America, 1981.

Moore, Kristin and Martha Burt. *Private Crisis, Public Cost: Policy Perspectives on Teenage Childbearing*. Baltimore, MD: Urban Institute Press, 1982. (Note: Offices of the Urban Institute are in Washington, DC, but publications should be ordered through the Urban Institute Press, 301-338-6951.)

Polit, Denise. *Building Self-Sufficiency: A Guide to Vocational and Employment Services for Teenage Mothers*. Jefferson City, MO: Humanalysis, 1986.

Quint, Janet C. and James A. Riccio. *The Challenge of Serving Pregnant and Parenting Teens: Lessons from Project Redirection*. New York: Manpower Demonstration Research Corporation, 1985. Other publications on Project Redirection also available from MDRC.

Sanders, Joelle. *Working with Teenage Fathers: Handbook for Program Development*. New York: Bank Street College of Education, Teen Fathers Collaboration, 1985.

Scott, Keith et al., eds. *Teenage Parents and Their Offspring*. New York: Grune and Stratton, 1981.

Smith Nickel, Phyllis and Holly Delaney. *Working with Teen Parents: A Survey of Promising Approaches*. Chicago: Family Resource Coalition, 1985.

Teenage Pregnancy: The Problem that Hasn't Gone Away. New York: Alan Guttmacher Institute, 1981.

Zellman, G. L. *The Responsibility of the Schools to Teenage Pregnancy and Parenthood*. Santa Monica, CA: Rand Corporation, 1981.

Zellman, G. L. *A Title IX Perspective on the Schools' Response to Teenage Pregnancy and Parenthood*. Santa Monica, CA: Rand Corporation, 1981.

General information about child care

Auerbach, Stevanne, ed. *Child Care: A Comprehensive Guide* (four-volume series). New York: Human Sciences Press, 1970s. Review of considerations and issues in planning child care; includes *Rationale for Child Care Services: Programs vs. Politics*, Vol. I, 1975; *Model Programs and Their Components*, Vol. II, 1976; *Creative Centers and Homes*, Vol. III, 1978; and *Special Needs and Services*, Vol. IV, 1979.

The Child Care Handbook: Needs, Programs, and Possibilities. Washington, DC: Children's Defense Fund, 1982. Discussion of the need for child care and the politics of arranging it; profiles of programs.

Franklin, Alfred White, ed. *Child Abuse: Prediction, Prevention, and Follow-up*. New York: Churchill Livingstone, 1977. Collection of papers on studies, current views, and legal aspects of child abuse.

Golub, Judith. *Child Care: A Review of the Issues*. New York: Public Agenda Foundation, 1982.

Johnson, Harriet M. *Children in "The Nursery School."* New York: Agathon Press, Inc., 1972. Goals and practices of a developmentally oriented program; no specific guidelines.

Levine, James A. *Day Care and the Public Schools: Profiles of Five Communities*. Newton, MA: Education Development Center, Inc., 1978. Different ways to provide day care in public schools; emphasis on the development, administration, dynamics, and trade-offs of each model.

Provence, Sally, Audrey Naylor, and June Patterson. *The Challenge of Daycare*. New Haven: Yale University Press, 1977. Study of an urban day care center, with discussion of parent relations; case studies, including some of teen parents.

Zigler, Edward and Edmund W. Gordon. *Day Care: Scientific and Social Policy Issues*. Boston: Auburn House Publishing Company, 1982. Collection of theoretical and social science articles.

Establishing and managing a child care center

Birckmayer, Jennifer and Anne Willis. *Guidelines for Day Care Programs for Migrant Infants and Toddlers*. Ithaca, NY: Cornell University Press, 1975. Advice on designing centers and programs; materials lists, routines, room arrangements.

Boguslowski, Dorothy B. *A Guide for Establishing and Operating Day Care Centers for Young Children*. New York: Child Welfare League of America, Inc., 1970.

Cataldo, Christine Z. *Infant and Toddler Programs: A Guide to Very Early Childhood Education*. Reading, MA: Addison-Wesley Publishing Company, 1983. Comprehensive paperback; deals with practical issues of staff, environment, administration, and activities; discusses program principles, history, approaches, and models; appendix includes early childhood competency profiles; can be useful in teaching child care.

Cherry, Clare, Barbara Harkness, and Kay Kuzma. *Nursery School and Day Care Center Management Guide*, rev. ed. Belmont, CA: David S. Lake Publishers, 1978. Excellent practical and detailed guide to management of programs for two- to six-year-olds; includes supply lists, safety and planning tips, and sample forms.

Dal Fabbro, Mario. *How to Make Children's Furniture and Play Equipment*. New York: McGraw-Hill Book Company, Inc., 1963. Lists materials needed and gives instructions and scale drawings for 60 projects.

Evans, E. Belle, George Saia, and Elmer A. Evans. *Designing a Day Care Center: How to Select, Design, and Develop a Day Care Environment*. Boston: Beacon Press, 1974. Detailed instructions, lists of materials, and drawings for designing, developing, furnishing, and renovating indoor environments.

Finn, Matia. *Fundraising for Early Childhood Programs*. Washington, DC: National Association for the Education of Young Children, 1982. Good, though short (76 pages in paperback) introduction describing sources and procedures, with references to more detailed materials and to helpful organizations.

Foa, Linda and Geri Brin. *Kids' Stuff*. New York: Pantheon Books, 1979. Catalogue of furniture, lights, and accessories for storage and for children's eating, sleeping, and playing; may be helpful as a reminder of the types of furnishings needed.

Greenfield, Patricia Marks and Edward Tronick. *Infant Curriculum: The Bromly-Heath Guide to the Care of Infants in Groups*, rev. ed. Santa Monica, CA: Goodyear Publishing Company, Inc., 1980. Developmentally oriented curriculum with discussion of values, discipline issues, and implementation.

Leavitt, Robin Lynn and Brenda Krause Eheart. *Toddler Day Care: A Guide to Responsive Caregiving*. Lexington, MA: Lexington Books, 1985. Developmentally oriented approach to the care of one- to three-year-olds, focusing on responding to individual children rather than on pre-school academic achievement; guide to directing play and behavior, assessing development, and relating to parents.

Lurie, Robert and Roger Neugebauer, eds. *Caring for Infants and Toddlers*. Redmond, WA: Child Care Information Exchange, 1982. Good introductory overview, with chapters on curriculum, health, parents, environment, staff, administration, and resources. Multivolume (out of print, 1986).

Manual on Organization, Financing, and Administration of Day Care Centers in New York City: For Community Groups, Their Lawyers and Other Advisors, 2nd ed. New York: Bank Street College of Education, 1971. Easy-to-follow detailed instructions and ideas for planning the environment and program, recruiting and hiring staff, setting up an accounting system, and managing the center; partially specific to New York and somewhat outdated but still useful with lesson plans, recipes, and ideas for cheap supplies. (This manual is not available for purchase any longer but may be found in libraries.)

O'Brien, Marion et al. *The Toddler Center: A Practical Guide to Day Care for One- and Two-Year-Olds*. Baltimore: University Park Press, 1979. Excellent, detailed guide to organizing space, time, staff, and funds; addresses potential problems, with troubleshooting ideas and emergency procedures; includes sample schedules, checklists, recording and report forms, equipment and supply lists, and activities; "Routines for Quality Care" give minute-by-minute instructions for teaching, supervising play, serving food, and organizing activities (out of print, 1986).

Overholt, Lyn and Tracy Barbra. *Exportability Manual: Rule High School Preschool/Parenting Learning Center.* Knoxville, TN: Rule High School, 1986. Describes development and operation of a school-based child care center; includes materials, recommendations, and detailed parenting and child care skills curriculum. The manual is available from Rule High School in Knoxville by calling (615) 544-1393.

Ruopp, Richard, et al. *A Day Care Guide for Administrators, Teachers, and Parents.* Cambridge, MA: MIT Press, 1973. Discussion of children, staff, directors, parents, program, and costs, with emphasis on management rather than on implementation and actual daily activities; models and case studies discussed at length.

Willis, Anne and Henry Ricciuti. *A Good Beginning for Babies: Guidelines for Group Care.* Washington, DC: National Association for the Education of Young Children, 1975. Written to help day care staff identify means to support positive growth in infants under fifteen months; statement of principles, guidelines, and procedural suggestions; discussion of the implications of daily events in a center for the experiences of children and staff.

Infant and toddler curricula and activities

Banet, B. et al. *The Scrap Book: A Collection of Activities for Preschoolers.* Ann Arbor: Perry Nursery School, 1972.

Bereiter, Carl and Siegfried Engelmann. *Teaching Disadvantaged Children in the Pre-School.* Englewood Cliffs, NJ: Prentice-Hall, Inc., 1966. Structured, academically oriented curriculum guide for three- to five-year-olds; aimed at lessening children's disadvantages.

Brown, Janet F., ed. *Curriculum Planning for Young Children.* Washington, DC: National Association for the Education of Young Children, 1982. Compilation of articles from NAEYC's journal, *Young Children*, addressing a wide variety of topics in a developmentally oriented and very practical manner; topics include play, multicultural education, the arts, and implementation of an effective curriculum.

Cole, Ann, et al. *I Saw a Purple Cow and 100 Other Recipes for Learning.* Boston: Little, Brown & Company, 1972. Activities for children who can read.

Forman, George F. and Fleet Hill. *Constructive Play: Applying Piaget in the Classroom.* Belmont, CA: Brooks/Cole Publishing Company, a Division of Wadsworth, Inc., 1980. Focus on interactive play for two- to five-year-olds using inexpensive materials; discussion of goals and developmental progress.

Gordon, I.J. *Baby Learning Through Baby Play: A Parent's Guide for the First Two Years.* New York: St. Martin's Press, 1970.

Gordon, I.J., B. Guinagh, and R.E. Jester. *Child Learning Through Child Play: Learning Activities for Two- & Three-Year-Olds.* New York: St. Martin's Press, 1972.

Greenfield, Patricia Marks and Edward Tronick. *Infant Curriculum: The Bromly-Heath Guide to the Care of Infants in Groups*, rev. ed. Santa Monica, CA: Goodyear Publishing Company, Inc., 1980. Developmentally oriented curriculum with discussion of values, discipline issues, and implementation.

Hawaiian Early Learning Profile (HELP). VORT Corporation, P.O. Box 60880, Palo Alto, CA 94306, (415) 322-8282. Assessment, curriculum visual tracking tool; covers cognitive, language, fine motor, gross motor, social, and self-help development from birth to three years old in monthly increments. Supplemental materials available, including *HELP Activity Guide* and *Developmental Parenting Guide*.

Honig, Alice S. and J. Ronald Lally. *Infant Caregiving: A Design for Training*. Syracuse, NY: Syracuse University Press, 1981. Comprehensive paperback guide that presents methods, materials, and strategies to help train caregivers; focuses on the child-development aspects of a caregiver's work.

Jones, Elizabeth. *Supporting the Growth of Infants, Toddlers and Parents*. Pasadena, CA: Pacific Oaks College, 1979.

Karnes, Merle B. *You and Your Small Wonder: Activities for Busy Parents and Babies*. Circle Pines, MN: American Guidance Services, Inc., 1982. Distributed by Random House. Two volumes, the first for birth to 18 months, the second for 18 to 36 months. Directed at parents; simple ideas for activities in kitchen, bath, stores, etc.; health and safety tips.

Krajicek, M. et al. *Stimulation Activities Guide for Children from Birth to 5 Years*. Denver: JFK Child Development Center, University of Colorado Medical Center, 1973.

Meier, John H. and Paula J. Malone. *Facilitating Children's Development: A Systemic Guide for Open Learning, Vol. I: Infant and Toddler Learning Episodes*. Baltimore, University Park Press, 1979. Sequence of learning episodes to be used in designing programs for normal or developmentally handicapped children; guides for parent learning and for evaluating developmental progress.

Newson, John and Elizabeth Newson. *Toys and Playthings*. New York: Pantheon Books, 1979. Role of toys and play in development, infancy through early childhood; recommendations of toys for appropriate ages, as well as how to use toys for developmental assessment and remedially; toys for handicapped and sick children.

Oppenheim, Joanne F. *Kids and Play*. New York: Ballantine Books, 1984. Games, activities, toys, and equipment (to buy or make).

Painter, G. *Teach Your Baby*. New York: Simon & Schuster, 1971. Developmental approach to activities for infants to three-year-olds; may be used as part of instruction in child development or for activities ideas.

Scargall, Jeanne. *1001 Ways to Have Fun With Children*. New York: Charles Scribner's Sons, 1973. Activities using simple materials for ages two to ten; games for car rides, sick times, rainy days, and parties.

Weikart, David P., et al. *The Cognitively Oriented Curriculum (A Framework for Pre-School Teachers)*. Washington, DC: National Association for the Education of Young Children, 1971. Primarily theoretical work; focuses on helping children to understand themselves and their relation to their environment; presents general goals illustrated by lesson plans.

Child development

Ames, Louis Bates, Frances L. Ilg, and Carol Chase Haber. *Your One-Year-Old: The Fun-Loving, Fussy 12- to 24-Month-Old*. New York: Dell Publishing Company, Inc. (A Delta Book), 1982.

Ames, Louis Bates and Frances L. Ilg. *Your Three-Year-Old: Friend or Enemy*. New York: Dell Publishing Company, Inc. (A Delta Book), 1976.

Ames, Louis Bates and Frances L. Ilg. *Your Two-Year-Old: Terrible or Tender*. New York: Dell Publishing Company, Inc. (A Delta Book), 1976.

Brazelton, T. Berry. *On Becoming a Family: The Growth of Attachment*. New York: Delacorte Press, 1981.

Dreikurs, Rudolf. *Children: The Challenge*. New York: Hawthorne Books, 1964.

Erikson, Erik H. *Childhood and Society*, 2nd ed. New York: W. W. Norton and Company, Inc., 1963.

Erikson, Erik H. *Identity and the Life Cycle*. Psychological Issues, Monograph #1. New York: International Universities Press, 1959.

Fraiberg, Selma H. *The Magic Years: Understanding and Handling the Problems of Early Childhood*. New York: Charles Scribner's Sons, 1959. Development during the first five years explained in simple terms; problems that arise at each developmental stage and how to deal with them; examples from author's career in therapy.

Freud, Anna. *The Writings of Anna Freud, Volume VI: Normality and Pathology in Childhood: Assessments of Development*. New York: International Universities Press, 1965.

Greenspan, Stanley. *Psychopathology and Adaptation in Infancy and Early Childhood*. New York: International Universities Press, 1981. Comprehensive approach to the diagnosis, treatment, and preventive intervention of psychopathology in infants and young children; characteristic behaviors and capacities of the normal and poorly adapted child at the different stages in early development.

Highberger, R. and C. Schramm. *Child Development for Day Care Workers*. Boston: Houghton-Mifflin Company, 1976.

Kaplan, Louis J. *Oneness and Separateness: From Infant to Individual*. New York: Simon and Schuster (A Touchstone Book), 1978. Description of Dr. Margaret S. Mahler's theories of early child development, which chart the baby's development from total dependence on the caregiver to relative independence and the feelings that parents often experience at the different stages.

Leach, Penelope. *Babyhood*, 2nd ed. New York: Alfred A. Knopf, 1983. Collection of hundreds of research studies about the latest research in early development, written for parents and professionals to help them make decisions about childrearing for their babies and toddlers; studies focus on physical, cognitive, and emotional development.

Mahler, Margaret, Fred Pine, and Anni Bergman. *The Psychological Birth of the Human Infant*. New York: Basic Books, 1975. Scientific report of the psychoanalytic research project that led to the formulation of Dr. Mahler's theories and stages of early child development, which describe the stages of emotional and psychological development from birth to three years and the child's different needs from the caregiver at each stage.

Piaget, Jean. *The Construction of Reality in the Child*. New York: Basic Books, 1954. Original research reports of Piaget, in which he describes how through observation of his own children, he discovered the stages of sensorimotor intelligence.

Piaget, Jean. "The Stages of Intellectual Development in the Child," in *Childhood Psychopathology*, Harrison and McDermoot, eds. New York: International Universities Press, 1970.

White, L. Burton. *The First Three Years of Life: A Guide to Physical, Emotional, and Intellectual Growth of Your Baby*. New York: Avon, 1984.

Health and nutrition for infants and toddlers

Boston Children's Medical Center and Richard I. Feinbloom, *The Child Health Encyclopedia: A Complete Guide for Parents*. New York: Delacorte Press, 1975. Health care, including diet, safety, first aid, childhood diseases and conditions, and an index of common emergencies.

Cohen, Stanley A. *Healthy Babies, Happy Kids*. New York: Delilah Books, 1982. Distributed by G.P. Putnam's Sons. Nutrition, health, common illnesses and problems, including allergies; easy-to-read paperback resource for parents and workers.

Fox, J. *Primary Health Care for the Young*. New York: McGraw-Hill, 1981. Comprehensive reference work; includes guidelines for preventive health care.

Lawson, Donna and Jean Conlon. *Superbaby Cookbook*. New York: Macmillan Publishing Company, Inc., 1974. Nutrition and menus for birth to 18 months.

Smith, Lendon. *Foods for Healthy Kids*. New York: McGraw-Hill Book Company, 1981. Nutrition from pregnancy to the child's puberty; emphasis on prevention, treatment, and cure of physical problems related to diet, e.g., hyperactivity, allergy; recipes.

Williams, Phyllis S. *Nourishing Your Unborn Child*, rev. ed. New York: Avon Books, 1982. Paperback with recipes and menus; also includes information on general prenatal care, pregnancy, and the development of the embryo into the fetus and baby.

Parent education and vocational training in child care

Barclay, Lisa K. *Infant Development*. New York: Holt, Rinehart, and Winston, 1985. Advanced textbook, with summary sections and discussion questions; designed for college courses; covers the development of intelligence, language, and perception beginning with conception.

Chase, Richard A., John J. Fisher III, and Richard R. Rubin, eds. *Your Baby: The First Wondrous Year*. New York: Collier Books (Macmillan Publishing Company), 1984. A Johnson & Johnson Child Development Publication. Very accessible paperback, informal in tone and with pictures; baby's development, guides for parenting, playing with baby, and designing baby's environment.

Child Care and Development, sets 1 and 2. New York: McGraw-Hill Films, 1972. (Price in 1986 was $138.) Set 2 consists of four cassette sound filmstrips: *Influences on Children, Intellectual Development of Children, Anxieties of Children,* and *Discipline and Punishment.*

Child Development Association National Credentialing Program. *CDA Competency Standards and Assessment System for Infant-Toddler Caregivers in Center-Based Programs*. Washington, DC, June 1984. Manual breaking down the skills necessary for child care workers; developmental approach to child care; specific examples of activities that create competency in caregivers working with children from birth to three years; emotional, cognitive, and physical development and health; discussion of issues of working with handicapped, bilingual, abused, and neglected children.

Colvin, Ralph W. and Esther M. Zaffiro, eds. *Preschool Education: A Handbook of the Training of Early Childhood Educators*. New York: Springer Publishing Co., 1974. Not a textbook, but a guide for those who will teach; theoretical foundations, general guidelines, special issues and considerations, and help in planning a training program.

Conger, Flora Stabler and Irene B. Rose. *Child Care Aide Skills*. New York: McGraw-Hill Book Company, Gregg Division, 1979. Beginning-level textbook; circumstances that might arise; instructions for supervising and teaching; ideas for child-care environment; lesson plans.

Cooper, John O. and Denzil Edge. *Parenting: Strategies and Educational Methods*. Columbus, OH: Charles E. Merrill Publishing Company, 1978. Directions for designing, developing, and implementing a parent-education program; focus on training parents to deal with common behavior problems.

Elkind, David and Irving B. Weiner. *Development of the Child*. New York: John Wiley & Sons, Inc., 1978. Textbook surveying growth and development from the prenatal period through adolescence, including normal and abnormal development and current research; well-written and formatted, with essays, biographical sections on researchers, and summary sections.

Fine, Michael J., ed. *Handbook on Parent Education*. New York: Academic Press Company, subsidiary of Harcourt Brace Jovanovich, 1980. Excellent work, with the history of, approaches to, and examples of programs for parent education; implementation and evaluation sections; chapter on training school-age parents.

Fleck, Henrietta. *Introduction to Nutrition*, 2nd ed. New York: Macmillan Company, 1971. Advanced textbook on general nutrition, with sections on nutrition for infants and children.

Levine, Milton L. and Jean H. Seligman. *The Parents' Encyclopedia of Infancy, Childhood and Adolescence*. New York: Thomas Y. Crowell Company, 1973. Reference work on physical and mental health; brief, simple entries on development, health, behavior, care, and guidance.

McDiarmid, Norma J., Mari A. Peterson, and James R. Sutherland. *Loving and Learning: Interacting with Your Child from Birth to Three*. New York: Harcourt Brace Jovanovich, 1975. Activities to stimulate learning; attention to psychological and motor skills development; does not assume prior knowledge, but density and vocabulary assume good reading ability.

Peairs, Lillian and Richard Peairs. *What Every Child Needs*. New York: Harper and Row, 1974. Comprehensive, dealing with emotional and physical aspects of parenting; easy-to-understand, practical advice on dealing with anger, discipline, toilet training, thumb-sucking, etc.

Pickarts, Evelyn and Jean Fargo. *Parent Education*. New York: Appleton-Century-Crofts, Educational Division, Meredith Corporation, 1971. General discussion of issues.

Princeton Center for Infancy. Frank Caplan, general ed. *Parents' Yellow Pages*. New York: Doubleday, 1978. Excellent, practical resource book, focusing on problems parents encounter; discussion of issues, as well as references to books and organizations; good section on first aid.

Princeton Center for Infancy. Frank Caplan, general ed. *The Parenting Advisor*. New York: Doubleday, 1978. Mixture of clear description of developmental theory and practical advice on childbirth, health, feeding, play, clothing, equipment, and discipline.

Wilson, LaVisa. *Caregiver Training for Child Care: A Multimedia Program*. Columbus, OH: Charles E. Merrill Publishing Company, 1977. Twelve sound filmstrips showing caregiving skills and behavior; accompanying paperback provides more information on the children and experiences; designed for those with limited background; does not address running a child care center.

Bibliographies and reference works

Bilingual Education: Early Childhood Education. Information packet listing journal articles, material resources, test resources, publishers and distributors, and resource organizations, associations, and foundations. Other bibliographies available as well, free of charge, from the National Clearinghouse for Bilingual Education, which is managed by Trevino, Inc., 4334 Farragut Street, Hyattsville, MD 20781. (301) 927–7085.

Garoogian, Andrew and Rhoda Garoogian. *Child Care Issues for Parents and Society: A Guide to Information Services.* Detroit: Gale Research Company, 1977. Annotated reference lists organized under subjects such as parenthood, child care, and child development. No longer current, but may be a useful guide.

Honig, Alice S. and Donna Sasse Wittmer. *Infant/Toddler Caregiving: An Annotated Bibliography.* ERIC Clearinghouse on Elementary and Early Childhood Education, College of Education, University of Illinois, 805 W. Pennsylvania Avenue, Urbana, IL 61801. (217) 333–1386. Published in 1982; includes references on caregiver training and curriculum materials, among other topics.

National Directory of Children and Youth Services, '86–'87. Produced by the American Association for Protecting Children (the children's division of American Humane) and Bookmakers Guild. Available from National Directory of Children and Youth Services, P.O. Box 1837, Longmont, CO 80502-1837, (303) 776–7539. Names, addresses, phone numbers, and managers of every social services agency, health department, and juvenile court/youth agency in every state, county, and independent city; listings of licensed service providers, federal children's program managers, national professional and advocacy organizations, and congressional committees responsible for social services, health, and juvenile justice legislation; guide to runaway youth shelters and federally funded resource centers and clearinghouses.

Subject bibliographies of U.S. Government publications are available free of charge from the U.S. Government Printing Office, Superintendent of Documents, Washington, DC 20402. (202) 783–3238. Some of the bibliographies available include *Children and Youth*, *Day Care*, and *Child Abuse and Neglect*.

II. Periodicals (child care, pre-school education, and adolescent pregnancy and parenting)

Note: Periodicals that are published by organizations listed in Section III solely as membership benefits are not listed below, but are mentioned in the organization's citation. Addresses for organizations listed in Section III are not included below.

Adolescent Pregnancy Prevention Clearinghouse. Children's Defense Fund. Six issues/year. Compilation of current research findings, program descriptions, statistics, and recommendations. Previous issues available, including: *Preventing Children Having Children* (1985), *Adolescent Pregnancy: Whose Problem Is It?* (January 1986), *Adolescent Pregnancy: What the States Are Saying* (March 1986), *Building Health Programs for Teenagers* (May 1986), *Model Programs: Preventing Adolescent Pregnancy and Building Youth Self-Sufficiency* (July 1986), *Preventing Adolescent Pregnancy: What Schools Can Do* (September 1986), *Welfare and Teen Pregnancy: What Do We Know? What Do We Do?* (November 1986), *Adolescent Pregnancy: Anatomy of a Social Problem in Search of Comprehensive Solutions* (January 1987), and *Child Care: An Essential Service for Teen Parents* (March 1987).

Beginnings: The Magazine for Teachers of Young Children. Exchange Press, Inc., P.O. Box 2890, Redmond, WA 98073–9970. Quarterly. Each issue explores one topic. Previous issues available on such themes as "Make-Believe Play" and "Designing Indoor Spaces."

Caring for Infants and Toddlers. Resources for Child Care Management. Quarterly. Information on critical issues drawn from ideas and experiences of a network of caregivers.

Child Care News. Child Care Resource Center, Cambridge, MA. Monthly. Articles on current events and issues, health and safety, and curriculum issues.

Day Care and Early Education. Human Sciences Press, 72 Fifth Avenue, New York, NY 10011. (212) 243–6000. Quarterly. Articles on curricula, model programs, staff development, and public policy issues.

ERIC/EECE Bulletin. ERIC Clearinghouse on Elementary and Early Childhood Education. Quarterly; four pages long; brief articles on research, curricula, programs; notes on new publications and ERIC/EECE documents and services.

Exchange. Exchange Press, Inc., P.O. Box 2890, Redmond, WA 98073–9970. Six issues per year. For directors of child care centers. Ideas from other directors and from publications on professional growth, leadership, administration, organization, and current news.

Family Planning Perspectives. Bimonthly. Alan Guttmacher Institute. Current information on family planning and abortion provision, contraceptive development, reproductive rights, adolescent fertility, international population policy, and maternal health.

Protecting Children. Quarterly. American Association for Protecting Children. Information on programs, research, state activities, legislation, and conferences on child welfare.

Research Review. Research Review, P.O. Box 620, Lafayette, IN 47902–9989. Monthly. Reviews new publications and research on child development.

Report on Preschool Programs. Capitol Publications, Inc., 1101 King Street, Suite 444, Alexandria, VA 22314. (800) 847–7772; in VA: (703) 683–4100. Biweekly newsletter. Covers state and federal government programs and politics, funding, conferences, and current research and issues.

Young Children. National Association for the Education of Young Children. Bimonthly. Articles on research and current issues.

III. Resource organizations

Note: Many universities operate early education research centers, and the staffs of these centers may be willing to provide assistance in designing child care centers or to refer center organizers to other child care specialists.

Academy for Educational Development, School Services Division. Provides technical assistance, conducts research and evaluations, and publishes reports on school improvement policies and programs, including dropout prevention and adolescent pregnancy prevention programs. Operates *The Support Center for Educational Equity for Young Mothers*, which provides training and technical assistance to educators and policymakers on improving educational opportunities and economic chances for women who bore their first child as a teenager; research and reports on effective strategies.

School Services Division
Academy for Educational Development
680 Fifth Avenue
New York, NY 10019
(212) 397–0040

Alan Guttmacher Institute. Research, policy analysis, and public education organization. Primary source for national statistics for adolescent pregnancy.
111 Fifth Avenue
New York, NY 10003
(212) 254–5656

Bank Street College. Educational Resources on child development and child care; Bank Street's *Teen Fathers Collaboration* has resources for designing programs serving teen fathers and provides referral to agencies involved in vocational training, family planning, and employment opportunity services.
610 West 112 Street
New York, NY 10025
(212) 663–7200

California Child Care Resource and Referral Network. National network for referral to local child care resource and referral agencies.
809 Lincoln Way
San Francisco, CA 94122
(415) 661–1714

Center for Population Options. National organization with primary objective of reducing the incidence of unintended teenage pregnancy. Provides training in the development and implementation of family life education programs. Publications on life planning and sexuality education. Also operates *Support Center for School-Based Health Clinics*. The Support Center acts as a national resource for clinics. Sponsors programs to increase communication among practitioners, assists program developers and staff, and provides policy analysis and information on evaluation.
1012 14th Street, NW, Suite 1200
Washington, DC 20005
(202) 347–5700

Support Center for School Based Clinics
5650 Kirby Drive, Suite 203
Houston, TX 77005
(713) 664–7400

Child Care Action Campaign. Membership organization focusing on raising public consciousness of the need for expanded child care services, establishing a network of child care agencies, and disseminating information on establishing and operating child care centers and referral services. Members receive information sheets and a bimonthly newsletter. For brochure and list of information sheets send self-addressed stamped envelope.
99 Hudson Street, Room 1233
New York, NY 10013
(212) 334–9595

Child Care, Inc. Resource and referral agency for New York City area; publishes newsletter.
275 Seventh Avenue
New York, NY 10001
(212) 929–7604

Child Care Law Center. Nonprofit legal services organization; main objective is to use legal tools to foster the development of quality, affordable child care programs; statewide legal support center; provides technical assistance on regula-

tory and legislative issues; publishes newsletter and preventive law publications; operates Law and Policy Resources Bank.
625 Market Street, Suite 915
San Francisco, CA 94105
(415) 495–5498

Child Care Resource Center. Resource and referral agency for greater Boston area; provides workshops, support groups, and technical assistance in child care program development.
250 Stuart Street
Boston, MA 02116
and
552 Massachusetts Avenue
Cambridge, MA 02139
(617) 547–9861 for both offices
For publications contact Cambridge office.

Child Welfare League of America, Inc. Holds national conferences focusing on child advocacy; publishes publications on child welfare issues, including child care, child abuse, and youth services. Catalog available.
67 Irving Place
New York, NY 10003
(212) 254–7410
and
440 First Street, NW
Washington, DC 20001
(202) 638–2952
For publications:
300 Raritan Center Parkway
Edison, NJ 08818

Children's Defense Fund. National child advocacy and research organization; operates Adolescent Pregnancy Prevention Clearinghouse; monitors government activities; has information on subsidized care and federal and state policies; has wide array of publications. Resource list available.
122 C Street, NW
Washington, DC 20001
(202) 628–8787

Children's Research and Education Institute, Inc. Public education and public policy research organization; Teen Father and Infant and Toddler Caregiving Training.
80 Trowbridge Street
Cambridge, MA 02138
(617) 492–2229

Council on Interracial Books for Children. Operates the *Racism and Sexism Resource Center for Educators*. Resource for curriculum materials, posters, and books with multicultural characters, settings, and themes.
1841 Broadway
New York, NY 10023
(212) 757–5339

Educational Development Center. Operates projects in many areas of education, including child abuse prevention and adolescent health education; individual

projects may be able to provide information on model programs and curricula.
55 Chapel Street
Newton, MA 02160
(617) 969-7100

The Equality Center. Policy and research center on educational equity; specialists on Title IX compliance and working with state education departments on policy regarding pregnant and parenting teenagers.
220 I Street, NE, Suite 250
Washington, DC 20002
(202) 546-6706

ERIC Clearinghouse on Elementary and Early Childhood Education (ERIC/EECE). Part of nationwide information system; offers computer searches for resources in a topic area, e.g., child care, document citations and abstracts, and quarterly bulletin.
University of Illinois
College of Education
805 W. Pennsylvania Avenue
Urbana, IL 61801
(217) 333-1386

ERIC Clearinghouse on Urban Education (ERIC/CUE). See above citation. Publishes *Trends and Issues* series and *ERIC Digests*.
Box 40
Teachers College
Columbia University
New York, NY 10027
(212) 678-3433

Family Resource Coalition. Clearinghouse and networking center for family resource programs; sponsors conferences; provides technical assistance and training services; publishes *Family Resource Coalition Report* three times a year, for members; other publications and information packets available.
230 North Michigan Avenue, Room 1625
Chicago, IL 60601
(312) 726-4750

The Foundation Center. Clearinghouse for materials on private foundations; reference collections in New York, Washington, DC, Cleveland, and San Francisco; cooperating collections in 145 libraries nationwide; publications include *Foundation Directory* and *Corporate Foundation Profiles*, and are often available at public libraries. Central office:
79 Fifth Avenue
New York, NY 10003
(212) 620-4230

Information Center on Children's Cultures. Established to encourage an interest in and awareness of other cultures; operates library, gallery, classroom, and consulting service; resource center answers questions and provides bibliographies on over 100 countries and on topics such as music, clothing, and festivals.
Communications Department
U.S. Committee for UNICEF
331 East 38th Street
New York, NY 10016
(212) 686-5522

Manpower Demonstration Research Corporation (MDRC). Manages and evaluates large-scale demonstration projects designed to provide better knowledge for the formulation of policies targeting the economically disadvantaged; responsible for Project Redirection; provides technical assistance and resources to program operators.
3 Park Avenue
New York, NY 10016
(212) 532-3200

National Association for the Education of Young Children (NAEYC). Large, long-established organization; publishes professional books; sponsors outreach projects and annual national conference. Membership available in national organization only or through one of 280 local and state affiliate groups. Resource list available.
1834 Connecticut Avenue, NW
Washington, DC 20009
(202) 232-8777 or (800) 424-2460

National Committee for the Prevention of Child Abuse. Publications on how to prevent child abuse.
332 South Michigan Avenue, Suite 950
Chicago, IL 60604-4357
(312) 663-3520

NCPCA Publishing Department
P.O. Box 94283
Chicago, IL 60690

National Organization for Adolescent Pregnancy and Parenting (NOAPP). Network of organizations and individuals; promotes the development of state and regional coalitions; provides referral to local services; has funding information; cosponsors national conferences. Members receive quarterly newsletter, *NOAPP Network*.
P.O. Box 2365
Reston, VA 22090
(703) 435-3948

Parents Anonymous. Child abuse public education and treatment program; links individuals and national, state, and local organizations, operates toll-free hotline.
7120 Franklin Avenue
Los Angeles, CA 90046
(213) 371-3501
Toll free: (800) 421-0353; (800) 352-0386 in California

Planned Parenthood Federation of America. Publications in family planning and sex education; referral to local affiliates that have further resources.
810 Seventh Avenue, 7th Floor
New York, NY 10019
(212) 541-7800

Resources for Child Care Management. Offers conferences, workshops, training programs, and consultative services on design, implementation, management, evaluation, and financial management; publishes books and newsletters.
P.O. Box 669
Summit, NJ 07901
(201) 277-2689

Sex Desegregation Centers. Regional centers funded by the U.S. Department of Education. Produce publications and provide workshops on teenage pregnancy prevention, sexual harrassment, and opportunities in nontraditional careers; workshops target students, teachers, parents, and others in public school systems. For a listing of the centers, contact:
Division of Educational Support
State and Local Programs
U.S. Department of Education
(202) 732–4342.

Sex Information and Education Council of the U.S. (SIECUS). Operates library in human sexuality and sex education; produces bibliographies on specific subjects and monthly newsletter.
New York University
32 Washington Place
New York, NY 10003
(212) 673–3850

U.S. Department of Health, National Center for Health Statistics, Natality Division. Statistics on live births, national and by state and city.
3700 East West Highway
Hyattsville, MD 20782
(301) 436–8954

In School Together was designed by Christopher Holme and produced by the Publishing Center for Cultural Resources. The Publishing Center is a nonprofit organization founded in 1973 to help nonprofit educational institutions and associations become effective publishers. Its services, which now extend to over 150 organizations throughout the United States, are made possible by grants from public agencies and private foundations and corporate contributions. The Publishing Center is located in New York City.